DIGITAL MEDIA
IN THE MUSIC
CLASSROOM

JAMES CROSS

RHINEGOLD
EDUCATION

www.rhinegoldeducation.co.uk

First published 2012 in Great Britain by
Rhinegold Education
14–15 Berners Street
London W1T 3LJ

www.rhinegoldeducation.co.uk

© Rhinegold Education 2012
a division of Music Sales Limited

Digital Media in the Music Classroom
Order No. RHG404
ISBN: 978-1-78038-250-0

Exclusive Distributors:
Music Sales Limited
Distribution Centre, Newmarket Road
Bury St Edmunds, Suffolk, IP33 3YB, UK

Printed in the EU

CONTENTS

THE AUTHOR

James Cross is an Apple Distinguished Educator, and previously taught Music and Music Technology at a large comprehensive school in Sheffield, where he was also responsible for learning technologies across the whole school.

He has since worked with school leaders and teachers across the UK to transform learning with technology, has guest lectured on teacher training courses, and has worked as an education consultant for one of the UK's largest software companies. James currently works for MediaCore, a company that specialises in online video-based learning.

James is passionate about educational technology, and believes that great tools and ideas have the power to change learning forever.

ACKNOWLEDGEMENTS

Thanks to Michael Woodward, my Head of Department at High Storrs School, for giving me the space and encouragement to try out new techniques, ideas and technologies in the classroom.

COMPANION WEBSITE

Additional resources to accompany this book, including videos and other supplementary material, can be accessed online by visiting **www. rhinegoldeducation.co.uk/dm** and using the code **ZA6F3W**.

FOREWORD

Music teachers are now standing at a crossroads, in a landscape which is becoming ever more digital. Resources now come in multimedia forms; learning environments are often virtual; communication and collaboration frequently happen online; and assessment and recording require the use of appropriate technology. More than ever, music teachers need maps and guides to help them navigate in this exciting, but sometimes bewildering, landscape.

I first met James a few years ago, when I visited his school in Sheffield to conduct an interview on his use of social networking to support his work in music education. He had just returned from a holiday in New York and was keen to show me his latest acquisition. This was a device I had read about, but never seen before – an iPad. James was already thinking about ways in which he could use it to support teaching and learning.

What shines through here is a writer who is more than an ICT guru or evangelist. As a secondary school teacher, James has built up a real understanding of just what it is about the use of technology that engages and inspires students to make music. He is also all too aware of the real challenges facing teachers, which are often about more than purely technical obstacles. He addresses, for instance, the importance of working with technical support staff and senior leaders in schools, helping them to recognise and accept the potential that the responsible use of mobile devices and a less restrictive internet environment can provide.

Here is a book packed with new ideas and sound advice, helping you to harness the potential of digital media in the classroom and beyond, supported with a compelling collection of online media resources. This is a practical manual which should enthuse, empower and inspire music teachers for many years to come.

David Ashworth
Music education and ICT consultant; project leader for www.teachingmusic.org.uk

INTRODUCTION

In recent years, the world has seen huge advances in digital media and the way that people use it. From broadband to smartphones, from streaming music libraries to YouTube and from the iPad to social networking, the way that we communicate, enjoy media and go about our daily lives has changed dramatically.

In the past, both in and outside of schools, the term 'music technology' has mainly referred to recording equipment such as the multitrack sequencer, MIDI keyboard and the recording studio. Like the earliest recording inventions before them, these devices were revolutionary because they allowed for music to be recorded and distributed with greater ease, and they gave rise to the music industry as we know it today. As these technologies developed, the revolution continued and music-making with technology became available to all, including schools.

More recently, music technology has evolved to incorporate a much wider collection of technologies. Largely revolving around the internet, they allow people to share, discover and enjoy music on demand. They allow people to learn instruments, teach others and connect with a wide range of musicians. They allow artists to promote and distribute their work without the backing of a record label, and there are a growing number of musicians rising to fame via this route each year.

Musicians are using iPads as instruments in concert, almost any song is instantly available through mobile devices, and countless amateur musicians are sharing their work through YouTube every day. Thanks to digital media, music has changed forever and day by day it's becoming more shared, social and democratic than ever before.

The students in our music classrooms are a part of this world and their musical lives outside of school revolve heavily around technology, whether they're listening to tracks on their iPod, discovering new artists through their friends' Facebook feeds, or learning to play songs from YouTube videos. In their world, music and digital media are inextricably linked, and yet in the music classroom there's often still a divide between the two.

It's important to our students' musical learning that this divide is closed. Digital media needs to start being integrated into music in the classroom as it is in the wider world, and when this begins to happen it can have a huge effect on the ways that our students learn and enjoy music in the classroom.

A grounding in technology is now essential for every student, whether they wish to go on to study and make a living from music, or to enjoy it just as a hobby. In the past, the student who wanted to be a concert violinist could afford to give technology little attention. Now, however, they'll need to promote themselves as a musician online. They'll need to put together a website or blog, sharing their performances and networking with other musicians online to progress their career. When they apply for auditions, it's likely that their name will be browsed for online, and a good online presence is now an essential promotion tool for musicians.

This is a book for music teachers who would like to integrate exciting new technologies into the learning that happens in their classrooms. Each chapter gives a brief background of the technology being discussed and where it's useful, along with information to help you navigate the often confusing world of equipment and tools. Most of the value in this book, however, comes from the classroom ideas: simple, bite-sized strategies that you can work with straight away.

The book has been designed so that you can dip in and out of it for inspiration, trying ideas at a pace that suits you. It's been written to accommodate all music teachers, from those who have never tried to integrate digital media into their teaching, to those who use it regularly and would just like to try some new classroom ideas.

The main focus throughout the book is on the musical learning that digital media enables. Many of the ideas simply come down to effective teaching with a technological twist, along with a few new techniques that up until now haven't been possible. It's important that technology isn't just used for the sake of it; there must be a clear benefit to your students' learning, and the ideas in the book remain firmly focused on this.

The chapters ahead cover a wide range of digital media and it's likely that you will come across some that you've not heard of before. It's important to note that in the world of technology, there is always more than one way to achieve the same result. This is true with the ideas in this book; there will often be different ways of achieving the same goal using alternative technologies or techniques. The endless choice offered by digital media can be overwhelming, and you need to consider which options and ideas work best for you and your students.

The world of digital media is also a highly interconnected place, and between the chapters in this book there's an inevitable amount of overlap. Many of the lesson ideas make use of several of the technologies covered throughout the book, and have been placed into the chapter that feels most natural. The 'blogs' chapter on pages 85–94, for instance, contains suggestions on using digital video as part of a blog, and some of the classroom activities here are strongly linked to ideas from earlier in the book.

It's always inspiring to hear other teachers' stories, and this book also contains case studies that show how real teachers have been successful in integrating new technologies into their teaching. From blogging to mobile devices, these case studies show just how big an impact digital media can have on students' learning. It's interesting that each of these case studies feature a number of technologies, and it's often the case that once a teacher has seen the benefit of using digital media in their teaching, it quickly spreads to other areas of their practice.

Resourcing is frequently an issue in music departments and a lack of equipment can often seem like a barrier for music teachers who would like to use new technologies. While it's nice to be extremely well resourced, it isn't necessary. Many of the ideas contained ahead need little more than a computer and an internet connection. Students' own devices are also a powerful learning tool that schools can tap into, and advice is given on how to do this in a safe and beneficial way. With a little inspiration and a proactive attitude, you will be surprised by how much you can achieve.

In schools it can often be difficult for music teachers to innovate with digital media due to restrictions, whether these are technological or political. Towards the end of the book, guidance is given on how you can work around these issues, whether it's persuading a network manager to unblock YouTube in the music department, or making a case to school leadership for students' mobile devices to be used in the music classroom.

This book certainly doesn't argue that you should lock away the percussion trolley and trade instruments in for iPhones. Instead, it presents simple ideas that will help to bring into music lessons some of the exciting innovations that are a part of students' musical lives outside of school.

The best way for you to make use of this book is to read through it, pick a few initial ideas and try them out. Refine and adapt the ideas to suit your own classroom, projects and students, and then build on what works. It's far better to try out a few ideas at first and spend time refining them, rather than trying to do too much and becoming disillusioned.

Digital media can often seem intimidating and it's true that sometimes things can go wrong. This isn't something to be afraid of, and it's certainly not a reason to avoid giving it a try. The best mindset to have is one of adventure: music has become so much more exciting thanks to technology, and by bringing these innovations into the classroom in a meaningful way, you can make a huge difference to the musical experiences of young people.

DIGITAL VIDEO

From *Sesame Street* to the Open University, video has long been accepted as a powerful tool for learning. However in the past, teachers who wanted to use it in the classroom have often found it to be too expensive, fiddly and time consuming to use regularly as a teaching tool. Technology has moved on considerably in the past few years though: we're now in the age of YouTube, cheap instant video cameras and editing that takes just a few clicks. Many classrooms now also have an interactive whiteboard at the front, providing a quick and easy way to watch videos just moments after they are filmed.

The aim of this chapter isn't to bamboozle you with technical terms, or to describe the latest video-camera innovations. Technology has evolved to the point where it can now largely step out of the way and allow the learning to come to the forefront. When we think about what constitutes great music teaching, technology rarely comes into the equation; it's the human aspects that are often most important, such as the interaction and connection with students, the friendly advice and the guided discussion. Digital video enhances these aspects of great music teaching, allowing the activities that take place in the classroom to be captured, considered and discussed in a meaningful way that genuinely adds value to the learning.

Due to its previously difficult nature, using video in the classroom can be a daunting idea for some music teachers, but those who do try it usually find that it increases student engagement, improves retention of concepts and raises attainment in every area of teaching. Many of the classroom ideas discussed here will seem like common sense, and that's where their power lies. It's the learning and not the technology that's the focus. With the Assessment for Learning strategies for instance, it's teacher-led discussion and peer assessment that make the difference; the video and technology serve to enable it.

All of the ideas ahead work best when the video can be shared safely with students online, and this is covered – along with a few other technical aspects and general tips – towards the end of the chapter.

USING VIDEO TO ASSESS

All too often, great musical performances and compositions from the classroom can disappear from memory once the bell rings. When working on projects that span a number of weeks, it can be difficult for students to remember exactly what they were doing the previous week, what progress they made and what they need to focus on during the current lesson. This can impact on progress, with practical time during lessons being wasted as students cover old ground trying to find their focus.

Anybody who's ever tried to lose weight will know that there's one thing that can increase motivation more than anything else: seeing progress on the weighing scales. The same is true for students in the music classroom. If they can clearly see that their hard work is paying off and that they're making real progress, their motivation and engagement improves. The techniques described in this section act as the weighing scales of the music classroom – a regular checkpoint where students can gauge and celebrate their progress.

 CLASSROOM IDEA

VIDEO STARTERS AND PLENARIES

1. As students work on a project, simply circulate the classroom towards the end of the lesson and quickly take work-in-progress videos that capture their progress so far.

2. At the start of the next lesson, play these videos back to the class as a starter activity. As students watch them, ask them to think about the progress that they made during the previous lesson.

3. Following on from this, ask them to come up with two or three key objectives that they'll be focusing on during the lesson. They may need some guidance on choosing suitable aims at first, and it can be useful to give students a few key areas that relate to the project, which they can use to devise their objectives. This is a valuable teaching opportunity that can be used to cover and discuss key musical vocabulary, performing techniques and listening skills.

4. At the end of the lesson (having taken some more video footage), play back students' work-in-progress from the current lesson as a plenary activity. Ask students to judge the progress that they've made against the objectives that they set themselves at the beginning of the lesson.

All of this should be done with copious amounts of teacher-led discussion and questioning, with prompts that encourage students to discuss specific elements of their performances, in line with the targets they identified earlier. Questions such as: 'How did their expression improve between the two performances?', and statements such as: 'Your group's timing is much better in the second performance – can you explain to the class how you achieved that?' are useful in guiding students' learning and listening.

It's important to keep these activities short and not allow them to eat into too much lesson time. At first, you might find that it's difficult to complete the starter and plenary activities efficiently, but you'll soon find that it becomes a natural part of the lesson and that students quickly become accustomed to working in this way.

This technique will need to be adapted according to the project and number of students in a class. For a project where a class is split into groups, it may well be possible to show every group's performance each time. However, when students are working individually this won't usually be possible, in which case it's best to film and show just a selection of students each time, and use those videos to draw up general objectives in discussion with the class.

 CLASSROOM IDEA

VIDEO AT PARENTS' EVENINGS

Parents' evenings usually revolve around grades and comments in the music teacher's mark book, but we know that mark books often don't always tell the whole story. Music is a practical subject and it's difficult to sum up a student's musical learning with National Curriculum levels alone. A music teacher armed with a laptop and videos of students' work and performances, on the other hand, is able to offer parents an engaging insight into their musical development, as well as back up their comments with specific examples.

It's often the case that parents have very little idea of exactly what their children are doing in music lessons, and they'll frequently express surprise at just how much music education has changed for the better since they were at school!

Using video to facilitate discussion with parents is especially effective at GCSE and A level, as it allows for specific examples to be viewed and for actions and targets to be discussed in a meaningful way. For example, if a student struggles to stay in time during ensemble performances, this can be shown to their parents and specific actions can be set to address the issue, such as practising at home to a backing track. Often, parents aren't musicians themselves; when they're able to see and hear what their students need to work on, they'll be able to support their learning in a much more effective way.

INSTRUCTIONAL VIDEO

One lunchtime a few years ago, I walked down the music corridor and heard a familiar piece being played on the piano. Looking through a door, I saw a student playing the theme from the film *Requiem for a Dream*. This was surprising for two reasons: firstly I didn't know that this particular student could play the piano (and he was playing rather well!), and secondly it wasn't an obvious choice of piece for a student to play, coming from a film that he was quite unlikely to have seen. I opened the door and asked him where he'd learnt to play it. 'YouTube, sir' was his reply. He'd been sent a link to a how-to-play video by a friend and had used this to learn the piece independently.

Online video sites have become a key learning tool for students. Searching for 'how to play' brings up over a million videos, showing everything from step-by-step instructions for playing popular songs and classical pieces, to instrumental and improvisation techniques. Interestingly, the majority of these videos have been created and uploaded by young people, keen to share their knowledge and benefit from the musical skills of others. With instant digital video sites such as YouTube and Vimeo, the internet has become a place where musical skill can be searched, shared and taught, completely on demand.

 CLASSROOM IDEA

VIDEO SCORES

Whether it's notation or guitar tab, many students find written music less accessible, and it often presents a barrier that can hold back their progress in music lessons. Of course, reading notation is still an important skill and the suggestion here certainly isn't that it should be ignored. This is simply a case of supporting different students (who learn in different ways) to make progress in their music-making; some students just need to see and hear music being played in order to pick it up themselves.

1. Break a piece down into clear sections.

2. Position the camera so that your students watching can easily see and hear what is being played. On a keyboard, for instance, a view that clearly shows the keys is most useful.

3. Record yourself playing the different sections. Playing in a slightly slow and exaggerated manner can help students to see what's going on.

4. It can also be useful to provide a narration that gives students pointers in what to look out for and focus on. For example, 'This is the middle section, which can be a bit tricky. Be careful to look at the fingers that I'm using, as that'll help you out'.

5. As with all of the ideas in this chapter, editing the video can be useful, as it will result in a neater end product – but in reality (considering the hectic lives of music teachers), this is an optional extra rather than a necessity.

6. Upload the video to a safe space (such as your VLE) for students to watch and download.

The use of video scores can make a real difference when students are able to access these resources using mobile devices, both during and outside of lessons. The 'mobile devices' chapter on page 62 discusses the practical application of this idea in more detail.

ONLINE RESOURCE

An example video score is available to watch on the book website. Visit www.rhinegoldeducation.co.uk/dm and use the code ZA6F3W.

 CLASSROOM IDEA

EXPLANATION VIDEOS

When it comes to revision time, or when explaining new concepts, common teaching aids in the music classroom are the information sheet and PowerPoint. While these are useful tools in supporting learning in the classroom, they don't fare so well once the student goes home. It would be great if students studied every worksheet or PowerPoint after a lesson, but in reality this isn't high on the agenda of the average 15-year-old.

PowerPoint files also lose some of the elements that help to make music lessons engaging: the connection, humour, pace and (most importantly) the music. In comparison, it's quick and easy to create engaging videos that retain the human element of music teaching, which means the learning can be so much more powerful.

1. Pick a single, clear concept to explain. It's best to keep each video short and sweet, so you end up with a selection of brief videos that cover bitesize topics, rather than creating one longer video that students are unlikely to watch all the way through.

2. Explain the concept just as you would in the classroom, using lots of musical examples and diagrams on the whiteboard to get your point across.

3. Upload your videos to an online space for students to access, such as a VLE or a blog. You could even upload your videos to YouTube, where they'll be available to music students across the world. Music teachers who have done this have often found that it's a rewarding experience, and there's an example of this in the case study on pages 92–94.

FLIPPING THE CLASSROOM

Typically, students learn content in a teacher-led way in the classroom and they are then set homework tasks to solidify their understanding. The idea of flipping the classroom turns this existing model of learning on its head, allowing students to learn the content at home and then spend their lessons applying it practically. This idea in itself could fill a whole book, but there are elements of the flipped model that you can quickly integrate into your practice.

The ideas we've looked at so far have been teacher-led, with the music teacher creating content for students to use in their learning. Student-led video work can be just as powerful, as it allows students to demonstrate and record their learning, as well as helping them to cement their understanding of key musical concepts. As mentioned earlier, many musical YouTube videos have been produced by young people; creating this type of content is something that students find both useful and rewarding.

With GCSE Music being mostly practical, it can be difficult for some students to approach the more theoretical elements of the course. Using video to make these areas more practical, and allowing students to use creativity and digital tools to demonstrate their knowledge and understanding, is a great way of encouraging engagement during a lesson. When students know that they'll need to explain something later on to camera, it's amazing how their focus suddenly improves!

As well as the initial benefits in learning the material, this technique also gives students a bank of videos in which they and their classmates explain key concepts. When it comes to revision time, this is often more engaging and entertaining than notes or a revision book.

 CLASSROOM IDEA

STUDENT-CREATED REVISION VIDEOS

At the start of a lesson, tell students that at the end of it they'll be split into groups and will have to teach a key concept to the camera. Not telling them which concept each group will be teaching will help to keep their attention throughout the lesson, ensuring they listen to all of the material and not just the part that they'll be explaining!

1. Teach the content as you normally would.
2. Later in the lesson, split the students into groups and give each group a single, clear concept to explain.
3. If you have enough cameras, give each group one and tell them that they need to explain their concept to the camera. If you only have one camera, tell your groups that at a certain time you'll be coming round to film their explanation.
4. Encourage your students to explain the concept in their own words, and to use musical examples to demonstrate their points.
5. Upload the videos to a safe space, where students can access them to recap their knowledge or revise.
6. Watch the videos back as a starter activity in the next lesson. This can be a great way for your students to recap their knowledge, and it also allows you to discuss and address any gaps in their understanding.

USING VIDEO AS A MUSICAL TOOL

With the reach of YouTube spreading so far and wide, some highly creative approaches to using it are emerging from imaginative musicians. A number of 'YouTube orchestras' have been formed, with musicians from across the globe contributing to large-scale performances through online video. As part of these performances, users are provided with either a traditional score or a set of musical instructions. They then film themselves playing their part and upload it to a special channel on YouTube, which collates musicians' contributions from around the world. The 'performance' is created when these responses are edited together to form a whole piece, which is also uploaded to YouTube for the contributors to enjoy. The idea that follows brings the excitement of this way of working into the classroom.

 CLASSROOM IDEA

VIDEO SOUND COLLAGE

1. Using a variety of instruments, ask students (either individually or in groups) to devise or improvise a short piece of music based on the following set of instructions:

- Sing or play something in the key of B♭ major (you can substitute another key if you like, but everyone must play in the same one).
- Simple, floating textures work best, with no obvious beat or groove.
- Leave lots of silence in-between phrases.
- Thick chords or low instruments don't work particularly well.
- Sing or play at a low volume.
- Contributions must be around 1–2 minutes in length.

2. After giving students some time to devise their contributions, circulate and record them with a video camera.

3. Load these video files onto the computer, open as many of the video files as you can fit on the screen and arrange them so that they're all visible (this can be a little fiddly to do, but it's worth it). Play the contributions in any order, stopping and starting them at different points. This creates a musical soundscape or collage from your students' contributions.

4. Allow students to come up and have a go at mixing the collage by stopping and starting videos at different points, and by changing the volume of them during playback.

The results of this activity can be quite beautiful, and students are often surprised at how well the different parts combine. This can lead to a great discussion on why the parts fit together so well, and because each performance is so unique and features students on video, classes feel a great sense of ownership over the end result.

For an example of how powerful this idea can be in practice, visit www.inbflat. net (a site created by Darren Solomon, from whom this classroom idea was adapted with kind permission).

ONLINE RESOURCE

Video guides that demonstrate how to create a video sound collage with iMovie and Windows Movie Maker are provided on the book website.

USING YOUTUBE COVER VERSIONS OF SONGS

YouTube has quickly become one of the main methods for amateur musicians to share their output. Searching for 'cover version' brings up millions of hits and the quality of many of these performances is impressive. The diversity of cover versions being uploaded by musicians across the world is also incredible, from ukulele versions of Britney Spears, to string-quartet arrangements of Lady Gaga, to piano versions of heavy-metal classics.

Such videos are particularly useful during lessons that follow the Musical Futures approach, as they help to open up students' minds to the creative possibilities available to them as they're working on their own cover versions. It's especially helpful if you select cover versions of songs that are likely to be known by students, as they're then able to compare them to the original version more easily.

One of the main aims of music education is to give students a taste of the enjoyment and thrill of music-making. The amateur videos that are being uploaded to YouTube in their thousands each day offer students a window into how people are making and enjoying music across the world. This is the first time that such a resource has been available to students, and using these performances in lessons is a great way of giving them a taste of just how magical music-making can be.

 CLASSROOM IDEA

MUSIC DEPARTMENT TRAILERS
In many schools, it's becoming increasingly important for music departments to recruit steady numbers of students to their KS4–5 courses. Open evenings and concerts are great publicity for music departments, but they often don't give the

full picture of exactly what students will be doing if they embark on a music course.

With a digital video camera and some basic editing, it's easy to produce a 'trailer' for a particular course. This can then be shared online for prospective students and parents to watch, and can be shown at open evenings and other events.

1. During lessons, use a video camera to record some short clips of students working on different projects. Try to capture a wide cross-section of the types of activities that students undertake on a course.

2. Piece these videos together using a simple editing application such as iMovie or Windows Movie Maker (help on how to edit videos is given on page 25).

3. Some interview videos of current and ex-students describing what they enjoyed about their music courses is also a great addition. The key with these is to keep them fairly short, and to ask questions that are focused yet open-ended. A mix of responses to different questions works well. Questions such as 'What have you enjoyed most about your course?' or 'What's been the best moment of the course?' are effective.

4. Many editing apps allow for background music to be added to a video, along with titles and transition effects between clips. These can add to the video's effectiveness, but try not to go overboard on such effects as they can be quite distracting!

5. The end result should be no longer than 4–5 minutes in length. Usually, videos any longer than this won't be watched all the way through; with online videos, it's often a case of the shorter the better.

Depending on your school policies, you may need to seek parental permission before sharing videos publicly, although many schools now ask parents for general permission to use students' images in this way as part of their initial induction paperwork. It's essential for you to check with your school that this permission is in place.

It's worth approaching whoever looks after your school's main website to ask if your video can be featured on it, helping to ensure it is watched by as many prospective students and parents as possible.

CLASSROOM IDEA

VIDEO AS A BASIS FOR COMPOSITION

YouTube is awash with film excerpts, trailers and short films that make an excellent basis for composition. When studying film music, allowing students to compose along to a real piece of film increases engagement and allows them to share in the excitement that film composers feel when approaching a new project.

1. Find a suitable film clip on YouTube or Vimeo. In terms of content, it's worth taking a moment to consider what will really catch the attention of a particular class. Clips of a more popular nature will often appeal to older students, whereas more generic or cartoony clips with a simple story will appeal to younger ones. It's also important to think about the musical learning outcomes that you are aiming for when selecting a clip. If the aim is to explore how moods can be created, for instance, then it's important to find a clip that has a mood which students can really relate to. Generally, videos between 45–90 seconds work well for typical school projects.

2. It can be useful to draw up a timeline to help students consider their response to the video. This should identify the main points in the video that students are to consider when creating their compositions.

3. Continue with the composition task in the way that you normally would, either by importing the video into a sequencer or by asking students to devise an accompaniment using traditional instruments.

4. As students progress through the project, be sure to discuss musical techniques that they can use to make their compositions more effective. (The classroom idea on the next page explains how YouTube can be used to provide examples of film music for analysis and discussion.)

5. At the end of the project capture students' work, either by exporting it from the sequencer as an audio track, or by recording your students playing live. (An MP3 recorder is useful here; these are discussed in the 'digital audio' chapter on page 39.)

6. If you have access to an editing program such as iMovie, combine your students' compositions with the film clip to produce a finished video file that can be shown in school or uploaded online, for students to watch at home.

7. If you have a sequencing application (such as Cubase) that has the ability to

import video, this idea can be adapted to work as a computer-based composition task, with the video being played live as the student plays or inputs their composition.

Copyright needs to be considered here, but there are lots of high-quality amateur filmmakers using YouTube to share their work. With YouTube, it's possible to send a message to the creator of a particular video and more often than not, by mentioning that you'd like to use it as part of a music lesson, they'll be happy to give their permission for you to use the clip. Often a clip that's unknown to students can actually work better than a well-known one, encouraging more creativity as they don't have any previous knowledge of the music that accompanies the clip.

ONLINE RESOURCE

Video guides that demonstrate how to create a timeline for this project, and how to combine a student's finished composition with the film clip, are provided on the book website.

CLASSROOM IDEA

FILM CLIPS FOR ANALYSIS

The internet hosts an abundance of clips and trailers from commercial films, and more 'official' trailers are now being placed on sites like YouTube. This can be a goldmine of content when teaching music for film, as there's so much footage available. For example, when learning about a specific musical device (such as the tension-inducing pedal note), it's not too difficult to find a film clip or trailer that makes use of this device.

The short nature of such clips helps to increase engagement in lessons by giving your students multiple excerpts from films to watch and examine. The instant nature of the video also saves time for you, as you don't have to relentlessly fast-forward and rewind through DVDs to find specific sections to watch in lessons.

Such videos also work well when coupled with listening questions such as: 'Which musical device is used to create tension as the laser approaches the hero?', followed by: 'Describe another musical device that can be used to create tension'. This approach allows students to practise their listening skills while boosting their engagement with the addition of video.

CLASSROOM IDEA

CROSS-CURRICULAR WORK WITH DRAMA

Some of your other school departments (such as Drama, Dance and PE) are also likely to use digital video to document and assess students' progress. This can provide an opportunity for meaningful cross-curricular work that contributes to your students' engagement with composition. This idea is similar to the one above of using video as a basis for composition, but instead of a video that's been procured from the internet, students have to compose music for a drama performance from their own school.

Ask a colleague from the drama department if they've recorded on video any recent performances from their lessons. It can be especially useful for engagement if this performance is from the same year group as the students who are completing the composition task, and even better if it actually contains some of those students.

Although this approach takes a little forward planning, it's well worth it. Composing for something that's real and is part of the students' world increases engagement and interest in the task. This is all the more powerful when students know the performers (or are even performing themselves) in a particular video.

This idea can contribute further to cross-curricular work between the two departments; with a little forward planning, drama and music projects can be integrated in a potent way. For instance, if you know of a drama project in advance, a composition project can be planned ahead of time and integrated into the work being carried out in the drama department. This type of project could culminate in music and drama students physically rehearsing together, followed by a final performance of the collaborative work that can be video recorded and shared.

THE POWER OF SHARING STUDENTS' MUSICAL OUTPUT

The PS22 Chorus (named after a school district in New York) is a great example of how online sharing can make a difference to the quality of students' output and their engagement in music-making.

At first glance, this choir sounds just like any other district or local-authority ensemble; it's made up of children from different schools who rehearse and perform regularly. Their situation changed, however, when the choir leader started to share their recordings on YouTube. Their videos started to gain attention from viewers around the world and rapidly spread through the internet after being featured on major news and entertainment sites.

The choir (from a relatively unknown school district in Staten Island) has had millions of views on YouTube, and they've become well-known because of the quality of their output. The choir has even gone on to perform with the artists they've covered, being featured on high-profile national television performances in the USA.

It is well worth watching some of their video performances; it's inspiring to see the engagement and love of singing on the students' faces as they perform (search YouTube for 'PS22 Chorus' to bring up all of their videos). There's no doubt that this engagement is also a result of the attention their video performances receive; they're not just performing in a school choir, they're performing to the world.

All too often, school music exists in something of a bubble. Sharing students' performances and compositions online can make a groundbreaking difference to their engagement with music-making.

THE TECHNOLOGY

VIDEO CAMERAS

There are a large number of user-friendly video cameras on the market that can be bought fairly cheaply. For day-to-day use in the classroom, a flashy camera isn't necessary and a cheaper model will usually do the job perfectly. Music departments that buy and start using a video camera often quickly find that it's in high demand, and it's a better investment to buy a few cheaper models than one more expensive camera.

Most digital cameras also have a video function that is often more than sufficient for classroom recording, so it may be that you don't need to buy any equipment at all to give the ideas in this chapter a go.

It is worth looking out for the following features in a new camera:

- As few buttons and options as possible! When you are using a device in front of a class, simplicity and ease of use are important features in their own right. When browsing potential cameras, a key question to ask is: 'If I pick this up off my desk, how many buttons do I need to press to start recording?' Ideally, you should be able to do this in no more than two button presses (one to switch the camera on and another to start recording).

- An integrated USB arm is essential, as it means that no extra cables need to be carried around.

- Shockproof, rubber housing that can resist drops and knocks can help to make sure your investment lasts longer (especially if the camera is going to end up in your students' hands).

- The ability to expand the amount of storage space on a camera with digital cards is a useful feature. Each teacher in a department could potentially have their own digital card that they plug into the camera to record their own footage, which avoids the issue of the camera quickly being filled up with other teachers' recordings.

High Definition (HD) recording is currently a standard feature of video cameras, and while the extra clarity can be useful, it also means that file sizes can be larger. If videos are to be uploaded online or stored on your hard drive, it can often be worth selecting a slightly lower recording quality from the camera's settings if this option is available.

Other handheld devices such as iPods and iPads are now capable of recording (and editing) high-quality video, and these are well worth considering as their prices continue to drop. You'll find more discussion of how music departments can make use of these in the 'mobile devices' chapter on pages 55–71.

EDITING

As mentioned earlier, for most of the classroom ideas in this chapter a basic understanding of video editing can be helpful, but it isn't necessary (especially when considering the workload of the average music teacher). Free applications such as iMovie (which comes as standard with Macs) and Windows Movie Maker (the Windows equivalent) will more than meet most of your editing needs. Where editing is necessary, it's usually just a case of cutting out unnecessary parts of the video and joining together different sections, which can be done in a matter of minutes using either iMovie or Windows Movie Maker.

ONLINE RESOURCE

Video guides that demonstrate basic editing with iMovie and Windows Movie Maker are provided on the book website.

SHARING

Much of the power of digital video comes from its ability to be shared online. Your VLE is the natural place to share videos, as it's inherently secure and private to your school. However, there are also a few online sites that allow teachers to share video quickly and easily.

When sharing video, the first question to ask is whether you'd like to share it publicly or make it available only to the school community. This really depends on the type of content. For example, you might wish to share concert performances publicly, while keeping video work from lessons private to alleviate any worries about online bullying or child protection.

YouTube is by far the best place to share videos publicly, and it allows for schools to create their own channel to showcase their content. Be aware though that YouTube allows users to comment on videos, and as these comments are anonymous they can sometimes be unpleasant. If school videos are shared online via YouTube, it's essential that the commenting facility is either turned off or set so that new comments have to be moderated before going live.

ONLINE RESOURCE

A video guide to creating and maintaining your own school YouTube channel is provided on the book website.

YouTube offers the option to make a video private, which means that it is hidden from the main site and only people with the correct address can visit and view it. This can be a good way of safely sharing the occasional video. The site also now offers YouTube for Schools, which allows school technicians to restrict YouTube usage on the school network to only include educational content.

Vimeo is similar to YouTube but offers some extra features that are useful to teachers, and it often isn't blocked in schools to the same extent. If schools want to share videos safely on their VLE, Vimeo can be a useful tool as it gives control over where the videos can be embedded. A teacher, for instance, could specify that uploaded videos can only be embedded on their school's VLE or website –

making the video more secure. (The process of embedding is covered in the 'VLE' chapter on page 75.)

GENERAL TIPS FOR USING DIGITAL VIDEO

- E-safety is especially important to consider when using digital video. While YouTube is a great resource, it's not suitable for sharing general work from lessons, as uploaded videos are by default publicly viewable.

- Check your school's policy on recording students. Many schools now ask parents for permission to record students when they first enter the school, so you are likely to find that recording students for internal use only will not be a problem.

- Most schools now have a member of staff who's trained in e-safety, so if you have any questions or concerns they're often the best person to approach.

- It's best to use school equipment to record and store videos of students.

- When using video cameras in the classroom, make sure that expectations for behaviour are made clear to students from the beginning. It's normal to have a few issues at the start, but these do quickly subside as students start to see video recording as being a natural (and enjoyable) part of music lessons.

- It's especially important to put emphasis on the need for respect when students' performances are being played back on the interactive whiteboard. Some students can be nervous about appearing on screen, and a calm and respectful atmosphere in the classroom is essential if they're to feel comfortable with the process.

 CASE STUDY

CAROLINE DEARING, HEAD OF MUSIC AT ST. LOUIS CATHOLIC MIDDLE SCHOOL, SUFFOLK

Caroline Dearing makes extensive use of digital video in her classroom, and has found that it impacts significantly on her students' musical learning.

For the students in her classroom, being regularly recorded is a normal part of their learning. Caroline uses both a Flip video camera and the camera in her iPad to circulate the room and record students' progress, which she then uses as a basis for self- and peer-assessment.

Caroline has found that it's crucially important to make assessment criteria as clear as possible to students, and to ensure they know exactly what's expected of them, before video work begins:

'The aims have got to be clear; it's not just a case of watching themselves on video for the sake of it. So I always create assessment sheets, where they have to tick against statements that are true or not true, based on the aims of the project. It's important that they're looking for very specific things, such as 'How did the performers communicate with one another?'. It's important to train them to evaluate very specifically.'

This grounding in self-evaluation and musical terminology has led her students to be able to evaluate their own musical work effectively, and in most cases the comments they come up with are those that Caroline would have made herself. She explains that 'it's so much better and so much more powerful for them to actually see for themselves what the issues are, or to voice the strong points', than for the teacher to offer the kind of praise that 'can become a bit vapid after a while'.

Caroline offers some tips for music teachers wanting to try using digital technologies in their classrooms:

1. **Make it easy for yourself**. Caroline prefers the Flip camera, as it's so easy to use and the video can be shown instantly to students. Although she has a more complex camera that offers better recording quality, this rarely gets used as it's more time consuming to show and edit the video.
2. **Know your tools well**. New technologies and tools can seem intimidating so it's important to spend some time getting to grips with their functions before using them with a class. 'There's nothing worse than a teacher flapping around. A little practice goes a long way in making lessons run smoothly.'
3. **Get the students involved**. Involving students in the filming frees up the teacher to circulate, and gives students ownership over the video evaluation process. Caroline often gives her students specific tasks when recording (such as 'film the drummer during the chorus'), as this helps to develop students' listening skills and awareness.
4. **Foster an atmosphere of respect**. Caroline's class has clear expectations of how students should behave when using video. This involves having silence before, during and after performances, and watching respectfully when other students' performances are being played back.

(Skype interview with Caroline Dearing, 27th October 2011)

DIGITAL AUDIO

The music industry has seen a massive shift in recent years, which has stemmed from one simple change: music has broken free from physical formats such as the CD and cassette, becoming available as small MP3 files that can be downloaded and shared online. It's mainly young people that have driven this change, by sharing music files with each other through services like Napster; discovering new music through social networks like MySpace; and loading their iPods with thousands of tracks. High-street stores have been challenged by iTunes and Amazon, and online campaigns to get a surprising track (such as John Cage's *4'33"*) to the top of the charts have become common.

As broadband speeds rise and powerful mobile devices become more widespread, we're continuing to see the music landscape evolve at a rapid pace. Services like Spotify allow for large amounts of recorded music to be played (often for free) from any device. Budding artists are finding new ways of promoting themselves and their music online, and new models of distribution are being developed that don't rely soley on the giant record labels. The singer Adele, for instance, was signed as a result of her music being posted on MySpace, and Justin Bieber's rise to fame has been fuelled by his savvy use of social networking for the promotion of his music and brand.

The production of music itself has also become more democratic. In the past, a student who wanted to record music would have needed access to expensive equipment and advanced technical skills. In complete contrast, students can now record music to a high standard in their own bedrooms with easy-to-use, inexpensive (and often free) computer and mobile applications.

As a result of the vast changes that have occurred in the recording and distribution of music, there have been winners and losers. While large record labels have had to rethink their business models, many smaller labels and digital-media products have thrived. Niche genres that were previously inaccessible through mainstream music outlets are seeing a resurgence, and a number of new niche music festivals are emerging.

So what does this mean for the music classroom, and how can you take advantage of these changes to create powerful learning experiences?

The music classroom doesn't need to exist in a bubble; students have diverse musical lives outside of school, and in most cases digital media and the internet play a huge part in them. Credibility can play a significant role in student engagement and learning. By making use of some of the tools that your students regularly use outside of the music classroom, their investment in school music projects can increase vastly. The aim of this chapter is to provide you with some ideas based around recording and sharing audio that you can easily slot into your existing projects.

SHARING AUDIO ONLINE

You are probably familiar with the idea that the sound of the school bell acts as a kind of reset switch in students' minds. Regardless of what they're working on and how engaged they are, once the bell rings they can instantly forget all about it. If that bell also happens to signify the end of term, the effect is stronger still. When students return after a break, the learning that happened before it is sometimes long forgotten and time must be spent covering old ground. Making use of digital-audio technology that students are familiar with outside of school can help to address this issue.

In the past, recording equipment was usually expensive and bulky. In recent years, we've seen technology move on and we now have inexpensive, high-quality MP3 recorders that allow for files to be shared online with a few simple clicks. These are invaluable to music teachers as they make the process of recording and sharing great music a quick and easy affair.

 CLASSROOM IDEA

DOWNLOADS COMPETITION
The aim of this idea is to tap into the excitement and credibility of high-profile music competitions. From the race to Christmas number one to the high-profile chart battles that occur throughout the rest of the year, students are used to the role that downloads play in an artist's success.

This idea can work well with any project that culminates in a final piece of music, whether it's a composition or performance task. A handheld MP3 recorder is a useful tool here, as it makes the whole process quick and easy for the busy music teacher.

1. At the start of a project, tell students that their final creation will be recorded and shared online, with the amount of listens and downloads logged.
2. Tell students that the track that receives the most downloads will be the winner. Ask your students to come up with an alias, which will be used later to identify their piece when it's put online (to avoid publishing students' real names).
3. During the project, there are lots of teaching points that can be covered in the name of helping students to achieve success when their track goes online. For example with a songwriting project, students could be asked to listen to pop songs and identify the features that make them catchy, allowing aspects such as harmony, melody and structure to be covered. In a performance project, instrumental skills can be taught and discussed. The key here is to cover topics in a way that's directly relevant to your students' success in the task; if they can see that what's being covered will be of advantage to them, the competition element will fuel their engagement and interest in the material being taught.
4. At the end of the project, record your students' performances and upload them to a site like NUMU (covered in more detail on page 40). Pick a stretch of time such as two weeks, and tell students that at the end of this a winner will be announced based on the number of listens that each track receives.

If you have time, it can also be valuable to discuss how music is promoted. Asking students how they become aware of new artists and songs is especially interesting. Years ago, *Top of the Pops* and *Smash Hits* magazine would probably have been the answer, but you're now more likely to hear that they discover music through friends' Facebook updates!

Once their creation is available online, students may well be keen to actively promote their track through a social-media campaign, by asking their friends to listen to it. Schools' attitudes toward the use of social media vary wildly; while many schools will see the possibilities for learning through social networks, others may be a little more reticent due to the perceived risks. You will need to use your judgement when deciding whether it's sensible to encourage students to share their work on social networks in this way.

You may also decide that it would be better not to put some of your students' work online at all. While most students will be happy to have their work shared, the process might make some anxious or embarrassed, in which case it's best to allow them to discretely opt out. There's nothing to be gained from uploading a bad performance or one that might cause embarrassment.

Most of your students will probably enjoy a little constructive competition, but sometimes it's best to give less emphasis to the competitive element if you think it might not be well-received by a particular class. Where the project runs the risk of simply becoming a popularity contest rather than a musical one, you can stipulate that rather than the number of listens being counted, the number of thoughtful comments that outline what's musically effective about the song will decide the winner. Alternatively, it can also work well as a competition between classes (such as where whole-class performances are involved), which will reduce the likelihood of personal popularity contests.

To make the task as credible as possible, it's best to share the tracks on a space where they are publicly available, such as NUMU. Having a wider audience adds to the thrill and engagement for students, but if there are any concerns then you could use your VLE instead to share the tracks.

STREAMING MUSIC

Streaming music players represent a huge shift in the way that music is listened to and discovered. Previously, to listen to a piece of music you would have needed to have that particular audio file stored on your computer or iPod. If you didn't own it then you would have had to find and download the track before being able to play it.

These new services work in a different way: they have a constant internet connection to a library containing millions of tracks, which can be played instantly with the click of a button. The libraries of these services are vast, covering all types of music from rock and pop to world, folk and classical. Such services usually have free packages that are funded by advertising. However, it's worth noting that the functions of these accounts do tend to vary over time, so it's advisable to check the most recent terms before asking students to sign up to a service.

Spotify is the service that has come to dominate the streaming market, particularly in the UK. Because of its popularity, vast library and comprehensive sharing features, the ideas below will focus on this program. However, it's worth noting that the music contained on Spotify is (at the time of writing) licensed only for personal use, which means that it's not possible to use it for playback in the classroom. The ideas in this section revolve around creating links to Spotify content that students can then use on their own personal devices, such as a home computer or mobile phone.

ONLINE RESOURCE

Streaming music services tend to rise and fall in popularity and as a result can be quite transitory. However, there are a number of alternatives to Spotify that you may like to investigate, and a short video review of a few current alternatives is provided on the book website.
Visit www.rhinegoldeducation.co.uk/dm and use the code ZA6F3W.

CREATING AND SHARING PLAYLISTS

A playlist is a collection of tracks that are grouped together. Tracks from any artist or composer can be added to a playlist, which Spotify allows you to share with a simple weblink. When a student clicks on this link, the playlist opens up in their Spotify player and allows them to explore the tracks you've added. Students can then save the playlist, which means that it's instantly available to them in the future and will automatically update itself as you add new tracks.

Playlists are an ideal way of building up a listening library for students at GCSE, BTEC and A level. They can be created and added to gradually, so over time a comprehensive and targeted collection that's specific to your department can easily be formed.

ONLINE RESOURCE

A video guide to creating playlists in Spotify (including collaborative ones – see page 35) is provided on the book website.

 CLASSROOM IDEA

SUPPORTING COMPOSITION WITH MUSICAL EXAMPLES

Having access to such a huge library of music can be very useful when teaching composition. Students often end up composing in diverse styles and genres, and you may have previously found it difficult to support them with appropriate examples. Providing students with links to musical examples in Spotify can be a great help in allowing them to hear how others have employed the musical devices and ideas that they're experimenting with.

For example, if students are starting to explore dissonant harmonies, a playlist containing works that employ dissonance in various ways can quickly be created. Students can listen to this at home to inspire their musical curiosity and support them in developing their own style.

For students who are composing in a dance style, it can be useful to expose them to a variety of dance tracks from contrasting time periods. Students who are into dance often have a fairly limited knowledge of the genre, and you can quickly open their minds to new musical ideas by suggesting wider listening.

Students often find composition difficult and a particular challenge for many is finding inspiration for a starting point. By discussing students' musical tastes and experiences, you can quickly find tracks that will help them to find inspiration in the genres that they feel most comfortable with. A student who enjoys pop, for instance, can be guided to a few key tracks and a conversation about the structure, instrumentation and tonality of those tracks could then follow.

 CLASSROOM IDEA

HOMEWORK LISTENING TASKS

Setting listening tasks for homework can often be difficult when it requires students to have an audio copy of the piece being studied. As it is easy to share tracks from Spotify through a VLE or blog, you can set quick but valuable listening tasks for homework by combining Spotify links with VLE tools such as surveys and discussion forums.

1. In Spotify, select the tracks that you'd like students to listen to as part of the task and add these to a playlist. (Adding the date and a reference to the homework task in the title of the playlist is a good idea, such as 'Y11 9th Jan homework listening'.)

2. Post the link to this playlist on a VLE or blog for students to access from home.

3. Alongside this link, add the listening questions that you'd like students to consider. Most VLEs offer the ability to create surveys that allow you to collect answers from your students, and this can be a great way of collating their answers for discussion during the next lesson. Adding a discussion forum can turn the homework into a more social learning experience for students, and tips for doing this are discussed in the 'VLE' chapter on pages 80–81.

CLASSROOM IDEA

COLLABORATIVE PLAYLISTS

Usually only the creator of a playlist can add tracks to it, and whoever it is shared with can only listen to the tracks within it. However with collaborative playlists, students can add tracks to playlists themselves to build a shared collection of music. This can be useful for older students and it's a powerful tool for encouraging wider listening around a particular genre.

1. Set up a collaborative playlist.

2. Ask students to explore the content on Spotify and pick three tracks that are typical of the musical genre being studied. This could range from the Baroque dance suite to 1980s' electronica; the process of searching Spotify and hunting through the tracks to find suitable examples is a great exercise for students. It encourages them to use specific artists and composers in their search, and it hones their listening skills and recognition of key musical features as they try to distinguish whether or not a track is typical of the genre.

3. Once students have selected their tracks, they should add them to the collaborative playlist that you have set up and shared on a VLE or blog.

4. Create a discussion forum on your VLE, and ask students to each contribute a post that explains which musical features of their tracks resulted in them being added to the playlist. This exercise can often create heated debates over whether a piece is typical of a particular genre or style, contributing to students' understanding of key musical features.

5. This idea can be easily adapted to include other areas of the curriculum, such as musical devices, unusual instruments or world music.

TIPS FOR USING SPOTIFY

You'll need to ask students to download the software to their home computers, but in the case of Spotify this isn't usually an issue as it's completely free and widely known. You will often find that many students have it installed already. Before using the software you need to set up an account, but again this is free and easily done through the application itself.

In the case of set works, exam boards will sometimes specify a particular recording or edition. It's worth checking that the version on Spotify is the correct one, although usually you'll be able to find what you are looking for as the library is so vast.

CREATING PODCASTS

A podcast is rather like a mini radio show: it's usually an MP3 file that is shared online, which contains an informative or entertaining mixture of talking and music. It's a great way of sharing learning content with students, and it's a convenient way of producing content that students can consume on the go. Students typically listen to podcasts on their MP3 players, which means they can listen to learning content while travelling on the bus or sitting in their bedroom.

Podcasts are particularly suited to the music classroom as they allow for musical examples to be easily incorporated along with explanations. For teachers who haven't made a multimedia resource before, podcasts are an ideal way to break the ice as they're quick and easy to create and put online. To create a podcast, all you need is a sound editor (such as Audacity) and a microphone. Then you can just explain a concept to the microphone and save this as an MP3 file. More advanced editing would allow you to slot musical examples into the podcast.

ONLINE RESOURCE

A video guide to creating a podcast (including how to insert music examples) is provided on the book website.

Podcasts can be particularly effective when they're produced regularly and uploaded online to a blog for students to download and listen to. The 'blogs' chapter on pages 90–92 covers how you can share podcasts online, and the tools that enable you to do this for free.

 ## CLASSROOM IDEA

REVISION PODCASTS

Revision videos have previously been covered on pages 15–17 but revision podcasts, where learning content is presented in audio form, can be effective too. These can either be created by the teacher, presenting content that students will find useful in the run up to exams, or created by the students to demonstrate their knowledge, which again they can use for revision purposes when the time comes.

Podcasts are simple to create: all you need to do is explain a concept to the microphone and include some musical examples that demonstrate the concepts explained. The aim is for each podcast to be a self-contained mini lesson that covers a specific area of content from the specification. It can help to think of each podcast as a short informational radio show, and topics such as 'the evolution of dance music', 'cadences explained in under two minutes' and 'a brief guide to ornaments' tend to work very well, with suitable audio clips supported by teacher explanations.

The preparation required for this can be fairly minimal, as you can base your content on existing classroom materials and documents, rather than having to script or prepare anything in advance of recording the podcast. A few ideas for podcast content are given below.

LEARNING CADENCES

Students often find cadences difficult to grasp, especially when it comes to recognising them aurally. A great way of helping students to learn cadences is to provide them with a podcast that runs through each type, accompanied by a musical example. This can be easy for you to create as it's simply a case of sitting at a piano with a recording device, talking through the different cadences and playing an example of each. At the end of the podcast, throw in a short cadence quiz for students to practise with, by providing a few piano examples for students to identify while they listen.

IDENTIFYING MUSICAL FEATURES

When creating podcasts, it's possible to include extracts from recordings alongside speech. This makes them perfect for creating mini lessons that encourage students to identify musical features.

1. Pick two or three musical features that have been covered in class and briefly explain these on the podcast, to jog students' memories and help to cement the concepts. Include your own musical examples where possible (for example, a pedal note can be quickly demonstrated on a piano and included alongside a brief explanation).

2. After explaining the features, include some brief musical extracts (of around 20–30 seconds in length) that contain one or more of the features covered.

To avoid copyright issues, it's worth sticking to musical examples that are Creative Commons licensed when making podcasts for students. Sources of high-quality music that can legally be used and chopped up for this purpose are covered on pages 115–116. Exposing students to recordings they're unlikely to be familiar with can be good preparation for their listening exams.

The 'VLE' chapter on pages 73–83 covers the use of online tools such as discussion forums, surveys and quizzes alongside audio files. The podcast ideas work especially well when combined with interactive tools such as these, as they allow students to gain instant feedback on their work, and to discuss their findings and thoughts in a safe and moderated way.

FAMILIARISATION WITH MARK SCHEMES

When preparing for performance exams and composition assessment, it can be very useful for students to have a good idea of what's being assessed and how the mark scheme is applied. However, the language of mark schemes can often be too abstract for students, making it difficult for them to use it to help improve their work.

You are likely to have a bank of work that has been submitted for assessment in the past, along with the marks it received. This is a great resource that can be used to put together a podcast which helps to cement the application of the mark scheme.

1. Pick a specific course element (such as solo performance at GCSE) and source two or three performances that contrast with each other in terms of the marks awarded. Although these will be anonymous when included in the podcast, it's good practice to ask permission from the students involved before including them.

2. After each recording, talk through the marks received, being as specific as possible about the reasons for the marks awarded and using phrases from the mark scheme. The aim is to provide an engaging discussion that sheds light on how the mark scheme is applied during assessment.

3. At the very end of the podcast, it can be useful to include one or two extra examples that students can mark themselves. This can make for a great homework activity; after hearing the guidance and discussion from the beginning of the podcast, students can then assign their own marks to the subsequent recordings and bring these to their next lesson for discussion as a starter activity.

THE TECHNOLOGY

RECORDING AUDIO

When it comes to recording students' work as an audio file, there are two main options available to you: recording directly to a computer using a microphone, or using a handheld MP3 recorder that can then be plugged into a computer to transfer the recordings. Which option you go for will largely depend on your classroom circumstances. Teachers who always have quick and easy access to a laptop will often opt to cut out the middle man and record directly to the computer, whereas teachers in other situations (such as peripatetic teachers who travel between schools throughout the day) may prefer a small handheld MP3 recorder.

MP3 RECORDERS

These are usually about the size of a mobile phone, have one or two microphones at the top, and most models record on to memory cards (like digital cameras).

As with video cameras, it's usually a better investment to buy a few cheaper recorders than to buy one more expensive model, as they tend to be in high demand throughout a music department.

Some features that you should look out for are:

- The ability to select different recording levels. This allows you to adjust the sensitivity of the microphone to match the loudness of a particular instrument or situation. For example, a higher level of sensitivity would be needed when recording a flute compared to a rock band.

- The ability to save directly to MP3. Most recorders are able to do this, but there are some that only save to their own format, meaning that conversion or extra software is needed.

- Some recorders take rechargeable batteries, which can be more economical if you remember to charge them regularly.

- The type of microphone that's built into a recorder is an important consideration. For general classroom recording, omnidirectional microphones are useful as they pick up sound from all directions.

- Some recorders come with the ability to connect additional microphones, meaning that teachers with more advanced recording needs can plug in their existing recording equipment.

DIRECT TO COMPUTER

With a laptop, it's also possible to record directly to the computer in a relatively portable way (recording directly to computer is also the easiest way to record a podcast). This method has the advantage of cutting out the middle man, as recordings are made directly to the laptop's hard drive instead of an intermediary device such as an MP3 recorder. It also makes the storage and filing of recordings easier, as they can be given meaningful file names and put into folders straight away. The tracks on an MP3 recorder often have to be deciphered because they are usually given confusing filenames such as 'MP300045'.

Most laptop computers will have a built-in microphone, which can be adequate for very basic recording in quiet classroom conditions. A much better option is to invest in a microphone that can be plugged into the computer, which will give you a far better recording quality. There are two options for you here in terms of how these microphones are connected to and used with the computer.

The first option (which is often the cheapest) is to buy a microphone that plugs into the 'microphone in' socket of the computer's sound card. These microphones vary in quality and price, from a basic model with poor recording quality to a more expensive microphone with increased sensitivity.

The second option is a USB microphone, which plugs into the computer's USB port rather than the sound card. These microphones bypass the computer's sound card entirely, meaning that the low-quality sound system installed on the typical laptop doesn't impact on the quality of recordings. As the USB port of a computer provides enough power to operate more sensitive condenser microphones, studio-quality sound can be achieved through this method of recording.

OTHER HANDHELD DEVICES

iPods, iPhones and iPads can also record high-quality audio; these are discussed further in the 'mobile devices' chapter on pages 61–62. For schools that need to invest in recording equipment, the versatility of these mobile devices can make them an excellent purchase. Often, they cost little more than a decent MP3 recorder and are capable of so much more.

SHARING AUDIO

NUMU (www.numu.org.uk) is a website that provides a safe community where young people can showcase their music. NUMU offers a quick and easy way to share digital audio with students, while also encouraging students to safely upload their own work. The streaming of audio files makes it easy for students to listen to tracks that are uploaded to NUMU.

While it's certainly possible to share MP3 tracks on a VLE, NUMU's strength is that it has been built to emulate how things work in the music industry. The service revolves around the idea of schools having their own virtual record label, which pulls together all of the musical work from a particular school. You can create spaces for classes, ensembles or projects and quickly upload audio for students to access from home.

Students also have their own accounts, which they can use to upload their own musical creations. The number of listens is tracked and students are able to comment on each other's work in a safe and moderated way, bringing the social networking features that are so prevalent in the world of music into the classroom.

ONLINE RESOURCE

A video guide that covers how to create a NUMU record label (including how to upload tracks and maintain your space) is provided on the book website.

EDITING AUDIO

The editing that you are likely to need to do with audio is minimal. In the case of classroom recordings, it's often just a case of top and tailing the audio to delete any unwanted silence or noise at the beginning and end. For podcasting, editing is a little more involved (especially when you want to include musical examples as part of the recording), but it's still a relatively simple affair once the basics have been mastered.

Audacity is an ideal program for the simple audio editing that you will need to undertake. As it's a free piece of software, students can also download it at home for their own use, allowing them to use the skills they've learned in school to create their own audio content.

ONLINE RESOURCE

A video guide to basic audio editing with Audacity is provided on the book website.

INTERACTIVE WHITEBOARDS

Interactive whiteboards (IWBs) have become a standard piece of equipment in classrooms of all subject areas. How they're actually used tends to vary widely, from teachers using them simply to project PowerPoint files, to those using the interactive features to their full extent.

IWBs become most exciting when they're combined with other technologies. They're a window to the entire internet and all of the resources, tools and media that it holds. For a practical subject such as music, they are also a means of assessing students' progress in a highly visual way when combined with digital video and audio. An IWB is also a great tool for facilitating class discussions and peer assessment of students' progress; when built into schemes of work and lesson plans, they can make a real difference to students' musical learning.

This chapter explores some of the ways in which IWBs can add to the learning taking place in the music classroom. It aims to open up new ways in which you can work with your board, by combining the features of the IWB with other exciting technologies such as digital video and online tools.

Although the ideas in this chapter don't go into the specifics of how to carry out certain tasks on different types of board, online resources and tutorials are provided on the book website to accompany some of the ideas presented here. These cater for the two main brands of board in use across the UK.

If you do need help with the specifics of getting started with your board, it's well worth approaching whoever oversees the ICT provision in your school. Kitting out a school with IWBs is an expensive exercise and many schools have invested in extra help and support to accompany their acquisition.

CLASSROOM IDEA

VIDEO CONFERENCING

Up until recently, video conferencing wasn't something that was easily possible without expensive equipment, and even then it wasn't easy to use for busy teachers. Now that cheap webcams, innovative software and fast broadband connections have become available, video conferencing is something that you should be able to do quickly and easily.

The IWB makes it possible for video conferencing to be an immersive whole-class activity, opening up the classroom to musicians, ensembles and other music classrooms around the world.

1. The first step is to source another willing music teacher who'd like to try video conferencing. The 'professional development' chapter on pages 103–108 outlines some tools and ideas for connecting with other music educators.
2. Discuss your schemes of work and pick out a similar project that you're both able to run over the same half term. Schools that use the Musical Futures model, for instance, could both run the first phase of the project during the same half term, or you could even devise a new project that's specifically designed to be used with video conferencing.
3. At regular points throughout the project, schedule times at which the two classes will video conference and perform their work to each other via the board. This works well as part of a performance project, but composition projects can also work too.
4. Ask the two classes to offer feedback to each other in a structured and positive manner.

This idea can easily be adapted to bring professional musicians into the classroom, for example to give feedback to GCSE or A-level students who are preparing for recitals. As Skype is so ubiquitous and easy to use, you will often find that musicians are happy to contribute to students' learning in this way.

On a technical note, it's worth ensuring that before you make use of Skype in the classroom, you test the connection on the school network to weed out any issues. The security on school networks, along with the varying quality of internet connections in schools, can often throw up problems.

Video conferencing sessions should always be supervised by you, and depending on school policies it will usually be wise to inform parents of the project. It's also advisable to run the project past the school leadership team as well, and there is advice on how to pitch projects and ideas to school leaders on pages 109–113.

USING WEB TOOLS ON THE BOARD

One of the most exciting things about IWBs is that they're a window to the entire internet and the rich world of music-making resources that it contains. Online music tools are usually highly visual, which means they can be especially powerful when used in conjunction with an IWB and combined with the large touch screen that a board offers. Although these music-making tools are undeniably fun to play with, they can also be a useful teaching tool with a little careful thought, even when concerned with more traditional concepts such as notation.

ONLINE RESOURCE

A video guide that demonstrates how to upload and use web tools on the IWB is provided on the book website.
Visit www.rhinegoldeducation.co.uk/dm and use the code ZA6F3W.

 CLASSROOM IDEA

DRUM-MACHINE RHYTHMS

1. At the start of a lesson, load a drum machine onto the IWB (see for example the drum machine discussed on page 96).

2. As a starter activity, present students with some simple notated rhythms that are each a bar in length.

3. Ask students to come up to the board and recreate the notated rhythm using the drum machine. In essence, they're transferring the rhythm from one form of notation (the traditional notation you've given them) to another (the rhythm grid on the board), and this is a valuable way of cementing their understanding of note values and rhythms. The highly visual way in which the drum machine shows and plays rhythms can help students to picture how different note values fit with the pulse.

4. Ask the rest of the class to comment on whether the rhythm is correct. In doing this, they'll need to use both their ears and their eyes.

5. As each student comes up to add a rhythm, ask them to do so on another track; as the activity progresses, the patterns will layer up to create a composition.

 CLASSROOM IDEA

PENTATONIC SEQUENCER

This activity relies on the iNudge online tool, which is a step sequencer that allows compositions to be built up visually. It is a great tool to use with an IWB, as it's so tactile and the results are so effective. As with the previous drum-machine idea, the musical learning here comes not so much from the tool itself, but from the teacher-led discussion that surrounds its use.

1. Load iNudge onto the IWB (this tool is covered in greater detail on page 95).

2. Ask a student to come up to the board and click some blocks to create an initial ostinato.

3. Repeat this process by inviting other students to add different layers to the composition in the same way (ask each student to select a different instrument for their ostinato).

4. Before long, a composition will be built up that consists of a number of overlapping ostinatos created from different sounds. At this point, there are a number of interesting discussion points that can be used to draw attention to different musical concepts:

- Whichever blocks are clicked, the output always works harmonically, as the blocks are pentatonic in nature. This can lead to a discussion on pentatonic harmony, or even a composition project using traditional instruments based on the pentatonic scale.

- When students come up to the board to click the blocks, there will inevitably be different approaches, from the excited student who clicks a huge amount of blocks to the student who takes a more minimalist approach. This can lead to an interesting discussion about rhythm.

- By clicking a straight horizontal line of blocks using the bass instruments, it's possible to create a pedal note that underpins the composition. This can be a great way of explaining the concept of pedal notes as the sequencer makes it so visually apparent to students.

CREATING DRAG-AND-DROP INTERACTIVE RESOURCES

One of the simplest interactive resources that can be created using a board's built-in software is the drag-and-drop resource. These require students to come up to the board and use their fingers or the interactive pen to drag words and objects into categories or boxes. They make for great starter activities and even older students enjoy coming up to the board to move objects around.

As with all interactive resources, it's important to carefully tie this activity into the learning. Students shouldn't be coming up to the board for the sake of it; it's essential that you have a clear aim in mind for your students' learning. The following ideas demonstrate some of the ways in which drag-and-drop activities can be incorporated into your lessons.

ONLINE RESOURCE

A video guide to creating drag-and-drop resources is provided on the book website.

 ## CLASSROOM IDEA

DRAG AND DROP

- Ask students to drag pictures of musical instruments into categories. For example, when teaching the instruments of the orchestra, students can drag instruments into boxes for different orchestral sections. When teaching world music, students can drag instruments onto their respective areas of the map. This works particularly well when sound clips are used too, as it allows for students to hear as well as see the instruments that they're moving around.

- During a performance project, present students with a bank of words that describe areas they might like to focus on while rehearsing (such as timing, expression, accuracy and so on). In discussion with students, move these words around the screen to sort them in order of importance, based upon their observations of previous work. When combined with the digital video ideas from pages 12–13, this can be a great way of helping students to gain clarity and understanding of the areas they need to work on.

- Create a timeline on the board, with markers that show the structure of a set work for GCSE or A level. Cut out themes or sections from the work and save these as individual audio files (the video guide to audio editing on the book website demonstrates how to do this). As a class activity, listen to the audio files in turn and ask students to drag them into their corresponding places on the timeline. This can help students to picture fully the structure of a piece, and to identify how musical themes are repeated and developed throughout a work.

• The timeline idea can also be adapted for use with younger students, for example when looking at film or programme music. A timeline can be displayed on the board that sets out the main events in a simple short story. You can then add a number of audio clips alongside this, containing music of varying moods. Listening to these clips in turn, your students have to decide which clips should accompany which sections of the story, dragging them into place as they do so. This activity can lead to great class discussions about why each clip suits a different section of the story, allowing you to work teaching points about musical devices into an engaging activity.

ONLINE RESOURCE

A video guide that demonstrates how to create a timeline and carry out the set-work idea is provided on the book website. This process can also be adapted for the film/programme music idea.

EMBEDDING FILES AND MEDIA

Music teachers will often make use of a wide variety of media as part of their lessons, from MP3 files of world instruments to videos of student performances. It's important to keep up the pace when teaching, and having to hunt down a specific sound file or resource during a lesson can disrupt your students' learning.

Interactive whiteboards allow for media to be embedded directly into flipcharts along with other material, meaning that you are able to play sound and video files immediately without having to leave the whiteboard application. It's also possible to quickly link image files with audio files, so that when the image is clicked, the audio file is automatically played.

 CLASSROOM IDEA

WORLD-MUSIC INSTRUMENTS

This classroom idea presents an engaging tour of different world-music traditions and instruments. It can also lead to a composition project that's based on the features of these different traditions.

Before creating this flipchart, you'll need to source some images of world-music instruments and sound files to accompany them. Pages 115–116 cover the use of media files that can be used for this purpose without needing to worry about copyright.

1. Create a flipchart that shows a map of the world (the built-in resource banks that accompany IWB software can provide this in a few easy clicks).

2. To the edge of the map, add a number of photographs of world-music instruments from specific countries.

3. For each of these photographs, use the IWB software to link it to a media file, such as a video or audio file. When the image is clicked, the media file will automatically play (the drag-and-drop video guide on the book website demonstrates how to do this).

4. As a starter activity, ask students to click on the images to hear the attached recordings, and use these as a basis for discussion. Ask students where in the world they think these different instruments come from and discuss the reasons why. As a result of this discussion, ask students to drag the images to their corresponding places on the map (even when the images are moved, the media files will remain linked to them).

5. Once the images are in their correct places, listen to the audio clips again. Discuss the musical features of each, and make some notes on the board outlining the key features as clearly as possible.

6. As a group activity, ask students to create compositions that make use of the musical features identified during the starter. If you're planning to do this, some thought needs to go into the selection of traditions and audio clips, to ensure there are clear techniques and devices that students will be able to grasp and use in their own compositions.

7. If your students' compositions are then recorded, you could revisit the flipchart and replace the linked audio files with the students' own compositions. This could make for a great activity during the next lesson, as students listen back to the recorded performances and identify the features that have been used from different traditions.

EXPORTING LESSON CONTENT

In the past, content written on a traditional whiteboard was erased forever at the end of the music lesson, as the board needed to be cleared for the next lesson. The onus was on students to capture its contents efficiently, and this could often get in the way of learning as they were focused on copying, not understanding. IWBs, on the other hand, allow for the contents of a board to be saved and exported. When combined with a VLE, this allows for resources to be uploaded for students to access at a later date. IWB software commonly allows for flipcharts to be quickly exported as either PDF or image files, which can be opened on any computer (including mobile devices).

 CLASSROOM IDEA

EXPORTING CONTENT
There are many situations where it can be useful to store what's on the board and share it with students:

- You may have used the board to explain a musical concept using a combination of diagrams and text. When this is saved and made available online to students, it's a great resource for helping them to revisit the learning from a lesson. It's also useful for students who have missed a lesson and need to catch up. Elements of musical theory such as the circle of 5ths, key signatures and time signatures all work well when presented online in this way.

- When assessing and discussing students' performances or compositions as a class, the board is often used as a tool to help collate students' comments and observations. Exporting these and uploading them to a VLE is an easy way of capturing these observations, allowing students to make use of them when rehearsing or developing their compositions. They can even be uploaded alongside video or audio recordings from lessons, using the embedding techniques covered in the 'VLE' chapter on page 75.

- Where a timeline for film composition has been created on the board, this can be exported for students to refer to when composing. This can be especially useful where it's been annotated with notes generated from a class discussion on which musical devices might work well at various points. Where schools allow it, students could even use their mobile devices to view this resource when composing.

SOURCES OF READY-MADE CONTENT

The reality of being a busy music teacher means that the time to sit down and make impressive IWB resources is rarely available. However, there are many ready-made resources available for you to use and adapt to suit your own classrooms. These range from free resources that other music teachers have created and uploaded online, to commercially produced resources that often incorporate more interactivity.

The best sources of free, teacher-made resources are the online repositories provided by board manufacturers. The creators of the two main boards in use across the UK (Promethean and Smart) both provide an online resource bank, to which teachers from across the world upload resources. When using these banks, it's usually best to make sure that any searches are for UK resources only, as these will typically slot into existing lessons with the least adaptation (although there are gems to be found by teachers in other countries). The TES resources site is also a good source of IWB material and can be accessed at www.tes.co.uk.

Many music teachers find commercially available resources to be useful, and these are typically more interactive and flashy than teacher-created resources. These resources vary in price and quality, and before spending any money on them it's worth checking out the free resources first. Most commercial providers offer sample resources on their websites, and it's a good idea to check these out in a classroom situation before ordering.

USING A VISUALISER

A visualiser works in combination with an IWB, allowing live video to be projected onto the board in real time. It's essentially a video camera on a stick, and it's a useful tool to have in the music classroom.

 CLASSROOM IDEA

DEMONSTRATING INSTRUMENTAL TECHNIQUES

It can sometimes be difficult to visually demonstrate an instrumental technique to a large class. As discussed on page 14, some students find it difficult to make sense of notated scores, but once they've seen something demonstrated they're able to pick it up quickly. For example, as part of a keyboard performance project, you can effectively use a visualiser to help students make progress.

1. Position the visualiser over the piano, so that a portion of the keyboard is visible on the board's screen.

2. Slowly demonstrate a particular section, with clear and exaggerated movements to help students follow the fingerings and notes you are using.

3. As you circulate throughout the lesson, you'll often pick up on specific sections or aspects of a piece that students are struggling with. Rather than repeating the same instructions and advice to individual students, you can now use the visualiser to help the entire class at the same time.

Visualisers can also be useful when analysing scores, as they allow your copy to be clearly displayed on the board for the whole class to see. You are then able to annotate over the score, either in pencil directly onto the score or digitally using the board's annotation tools. This is particularly useful for those students who find score reading a challenge, as it allows them to make effective notes in their own scores and keep track of which section is being discussed. As mentioned above, annotated scores produced in this way can be exported as PDF files and uploaded to a VLE, for students to access at a later date.

ANNOTATING ON-SCREEN

IWBs offer the ability to digitally annotate over existing documents such as images, Word documents, PDFs and websites. You might find this particularly useful as it allows for resources such as music scores, mark schemes and past exam papers to be manipulated and added to on screen using the digital pen.

 CLASSROOM IDEA

ANNOTATION
Here are a few ideas for making use of the ability to annotate documents on the IWB:

- Annotate the score of a set work, using different colours to highlight how individual themes are used and developed within a section, or to show clearly the structure of the work in a visual way.

- Blank out sections of a score (you can do this by drawing a white box over a bar and adding in a blank stave using the line drawing tool), and ask students to fill in the blanks using the digital pen.

- Bring up a copy of the mark scheme for student performances, and use this to inform peer assessment and class discussion after students have performed in class. Use the annotation tools to highlight phrases and circle the awarded marks (once completed, you can export this and put it online for students to access later).

- Exam boards usually provide PDF copies of past papers, which can be loaded onto the screen and filled in digitally after a class discussion of each question. This way, an exemplar exam paper can be created by a whole class, then saved and uploaded to a VLE for use during revision.

 CLASSROOM IDEA

VIDEO SNAPSHOTS

The IWB allows you to present videos to an entire class quickly and easily, transforming video-based activities into an engaging cinema-like experience. However, going beyond the simple playing of video files, there are other ways in which the IWB can help you to assess students' progress through video. IWBs allow you to take snapshots from a video, which you can then annotate with the digital pen. By taking a number of snapshots at different points in the video, you can create a visual timeline that can be used to facilitate class discussion and jog students' memories of certain moments in the video.

Here are a few ideas for how this can be used in the music classroom:

- Take a snapshot from a video of a student performing in order to highlight their posture. For example, you could take a freeze frame of a student playing the violin and use the digital pen to show how they are slouching, by drawing a straight line onto the image. This can be a great help in drawing attention to students' stance and posture when performing, and once they've seen it visually they find it much easier to improve.

- At the start of a composition project that requires students to write music to accompany a film clip, you could take snapshots of the stimulus video to illustrate important points in the action. These can then be placed on a timeline, with the digital pen being used to jot down students' musical suggestions for each section as part of a class discussion.

- This timeline idea can be adapted to create a video listening activity for students. When watching a video of an orchestral performance, for instance, still snapshots can be pulled out of the video to illustrate a printed 'timeline quiz', with questions for students to answer as they watch the video on the board. Questions could be along the lines of: 'What type of scale are the bassoons playing at 1:34?', or 'Which technique does the pianist use at 2:40?'

Before annotating and discussing a video, it's usually best to let students watch it through once without interruption. This will give them a feel for the entire video, making the annotation and class discussion that follows more informed.

ONLINE RESOURCE

A video guide that demonstrates how to take and annotate snapshots is provided on the book website.

 CLASSROOM IDEA

ASSESSMENT FOR LEARNING

This activity is an extension of the Assessment for Learning idea in the 'digital video' chapter on page 12. In this case, it makes use of the interactive features of the IWB to solicit and collate students' responses to a class performance.

This idea revolves around a simple interactive resource that has a number of sliders on the screen, which can be moved along a scale of one to five. Each slider has a title that can be changed to show different assessment criteria.

1. After students have performed, load the slider onto the IWB.

2. Lead a class discussion of each piece of assessment criteria in turn. Ask students to offer their opinions on where along each scale the performance sits, and use the sliders to show the general consensus from students' responses.

3. The IWB is acting here as a facilitator for class discussion, giving a visual representation on which to frame the learning. Teacher-led discussion should draw out reasons for students' choices, and suggestions for how the performances can be improved next time.

It's important to keep this activity positive, soliciting praise from students as well as suggesting areas for improvement.

ONLINE RESOURCE

An example slider is provided on the book website, which can be quickly used to implement this idea and further tweaked to suit your own needs and projects.

MOBILE DEVICES

During a classroom group project I once spotted a student with his iPhone out, showing the screen to another classmate, and in line with the school rules I asked him to put it away. He held up the screen for me to see and on it was a guitar chord app. He was using this app to teach chords to another student in his group; his mobile phone was supporting his learning in a valuable way, by allowing him to teach one of his peers a new skill and helping his group to make better progress. Yet the school's rules on mobile devices expressly forbade their use in the classroom, effectively outlawing this powerful learning tool.

One of the biggest technological shifts in recent years has been the eruption of mobile devices into hands and pockets across the globe. To illustrate just how much things have changed from a music perspective, it's interesting to think back to what a typical studio looked like in the 1990s. Being prohibitively expensive, huge in size and complex in operation, studio recording wasn't easy for musicians to access, and in many cases studios certainly weren't something that schools could hope to afford. Software that replicated the equipment in these studios started to emerge in the mid-1990s, but it was still expensive and often required extra hardware and powerful computers to run.

Skip forward to today, and we find that the majority of students in the music classroom have the ability to record, mix and create music in their pockets. They also have full access to the internet, a huge collection of videos (thanks to websites such as YouTube) and a vast library of songs (through programs such as iTunes and Spotify).

However, the use of mobile devices in the school is still in its infancy. Although schools have experimented with various pieces of mobile technology in the past, previous devices (such as the PDA) failed to make any real impact on learning because the technology hadn't yet caught on outside of the school gates.

When Apple's iPhone launched, it vaulted mobile technologies into another league and handheld devices have since become one of the fastest growing categories of consumer electronics. The use of mobile devices and the range of tasks they can do is growing at an unprecedented rate, yet in many cases, schools are failing to see the potential that these devices hold for learning. Schools were once ahead of the general public in their experimentation with mobile technologies, but they're now quickly falling behind.

As an illustration of this divide, imagine the student that regularly makes music at home using his iPod Touch. He's downloaded a few drum-machine apps, and has used these to create backing tracks that he then records himself rapping over. As soon as it's finished, he publishes his music through his Facebook and YouTube accounts, where his friends and people across the world can listen to and comment on it. He's getting better too, and his tracks are getting more and more listens.

This same student then walks into school the next day, where his first lesson is a music class. His music teacher isn't aware of his passion for music-making, as he's never shown much interest during lessons and struggles with notation. All this time, his iPod stays in his pocket (as it will be confiscated if seen), meaning that he's not able to use the music-making device that he most identifies with. His musical life and identity are completely disconnected from his musical education.

There are a growing number of schools where students are each provided with their own handheld devices such as iPads, and a few music teachers will be lucky enough to have easy access to mobile devices. However, many music departments are in a position where expenditure is pushed to its limits, and buying sets of handhelds just isn't an option. Students' own devices are a powerful resource that shouldn't be ignored, and with careful management and a focus on the learning they can be usefully integrated into the classroom. Along with practical ideas for incorporating mobile devices into the music classroom, this chapter also explores how to manage student behaviour when using mobile devices, ensuring that their use enhances the learning in a positive way.

Attitudes toward the use of students' own devices for learning varies wildly across different schools. However, opinions are beginning to change as new possibilities for learning emerge, as evidenced by the 'bring your own device' (BYOD) movement, where students are encouraged to use their own devices for learning in a number of schools across the world. It's especially important to consider equality of access when thinking about adopting such an approach, as in the majority of school situations not every student will have access to their own handheld device.

Where departments do have funds to spend, the versatility of mobile devices can make them a sound investment. An iPod Touch, for example, is relatively affordable and with a little investment in apps and peripherals (which are explored later in this chapter), it can act as an internet browser, a video camera, a multitrack recorder, a drum machine, a virtual keyboard, a voting device, a guitar tuner and a virtual amplifier.

Of course, most of the functions available on a mobile device such as an iPad or iPod Touch are also available on a laptop or desktop computer, and the question of 'why not just use a computer?' often comes up when discussing the use of mobile devices in the classroom. The explosion of mobile devices into the mainstream market, along with their ever-increasing power and versatility, has signaled that the future of computing will be increasingly mobile. As this technology continues to evolve, more and more of these devices will inevitably find their way into schools, and it's exciting that the music classroom can be a part of this 'mobile revolution'. On a more practical note, mobile devices also have an obvious advantage when it comes to portability, giving them added flexibility in the classroom.

Whatever situation you find yourself in when it comes to mobile devices, this chapter aims to signpost the possibilities for learning. Whether it's a whole-class activity, or simply using a single iPad as a mobile recording device, the aim of this chapter is to give you some practical ideas for using mobile devices in your classroom.

INCORPORATING DEVICES INTO CLASSROOM MUSIC-MAKING

In the world of music-making, it is becoming easier to incorporate innovative technologies into performances that also make use of traditional instruments. Bjork is one artist who has used an iPad as part of her performances, and has released the album *Biophilia* as an iPad app. This allows users to interact with animations accompanying the music, remix it, and read musicological analyses of the album's tracks. YouTube is also awash with videos of iPad and iPhone instruments being played, and some musicians have even gone as far as creating 'iPad orchestras', in which each musician's iPad acts as a different instrument.

One of the most powerful features of handheld devices for music is that they're able to emulate a wide number of instruments and devices. Virtual guitars, drum kits and pianos are available, alongside faithful reproductions of drum machines, synthesisers and sequencers. In addition to this, there is a host of innovative instruments emerging in the form of apps, taking advantage of the processing power and touch screens that devices such as the iPad have to offer.

By being open-minded to the use of mobile devices alongside traditional instruments, you can open up a new world of sonic possibilities for students. This can be very effective for students who don't have existing instrumental skills, or are unable to access traditional instruments because of a disability.

 CLASSROOM IDEA

USING HANDHELD DEVICES AS PART OF GROUP WORK

- As part of a group performance project involving different instruments, a handheld device can be a great way of extending the instruments that are available to students. When performing popular songs, for instance, students will often have a need for instruments that aren't part of the department's resources, but the chances are they'll be able to find an app that allows them to play a virtual version of the instrument.

- Drum-machine apps can give students a solid foundation on which to base their group performances or compositions. At the start of a project, ask students to generate a simple drum beat that they can use as a basis for their performance or composition. It can be useful to discuss how an effective beat is created, and to listen to existing beats before students make their own. As always, focused questioning can help students here. Why does the bass drum sound on every beat? Can they hear any repeated patterns in any of the parts? What makes an effective drum-machine beat?

- Often, students who lack confidence or instrumental skills can find it difficult to engage fully with music-making in a group situation, and as a result they'll often withdraw from the activity or quickly go off the task. Finding a suitable touch-screen instrument for them to play can be a great way of engaging them in a task. This can also be especially useful for students who are restricted in their movements due to a disability, or who have other learning needs that mean they're not able to use traditional instruments confidently. The intuitive nature of mobile devices can go a long way in allowing and encouraging students to take part.

COMPOSING USING APPS

Apps aren't just useful for performance; they're also becoming more valuable for the creation of musical compositions. In the past, composition in music lessons has often involved MIDI keyboards and either sequencers such as Cubase or notation software like Sibelius. Music composition can make use of a much wider range of software than schools have previously had access to; the use of mobile apps allows schools to introduce new compositional tools into students' music-making.

DJ apps allow students to mix tracks and beats in a highly tactile and visual way by using a touch screen. Students' own tracks can be used (either ones they've composed themselves, or ones that have been taken from their personal collections), making activities more credible and tapping into students' own musical tastes and interests. DJ apps are covered in more detail later in the chapter on pages 63–64.

Composition apps such as FL Studio allow students to create arrangements directly on a mobile device, using credible sounds and effects to build up successful compositions.

Apps that present virtual versions of world-music instruments (such as the sitar) and music-technology equipment (such as a 1980s' drum machine) allow students to access and explore the musical possibilities of resources that previously may have been out of their reach.

DOCUMENTING MUSICAL LEARNING

Mobile phone footage is now a regular feature on the news. The rapid improvement in video quality, and the ability to share footage quickly and easily, has led to a surge in people using their mobile phones to record events. This is happening in the world of music, too. Go to any gig and you'll be likely to find a sea of mobile phones being held up to capture the proceedings.

Allowing students to use mobile devices to record and document the musical learning that takes place in the classroom can be a great way of fostering pride in their music-making. The vast majority of mobile devices (including the ones in students' pockets) are now capable of recording high-quality video, making it easy for students to document their learning. Because this footage is on students' own devices, it helps to give them ownership over the learning that's taking place.

Of course, careful thought is needed when allowing students to use their devices in this way, and a clear code of conduct and high expectations need to be set in place. As with the other ideas in this book, the focus should be on the learning: students must have a clearly defined objective when documenting their learning on their mobile devices.

This approach can be adapted to suit different classrooms and projects. If you don't feel it is suitable to allow students to film using their own devices (and in some cases it won't be), appoint one student to be the 'learning recorder' and allow them to use a school device. This can be a good way of documenting progress in a more controlled way.

 CLASSROOM IDEA

COLLECTING STUDENT RESPONSES AND FEEDBACK

Class sets of voting handsets are a resource that many schools see the value in, but few are able to afford them on a large scale. They're particularly useful for a subjective subject such as Music, which lends itself so well to Assessment for Learning strategies, as teachers often want to solicit students' opinions and thoughts.

Poll Everywhere (www.polleverywhere.com) allows you to quickly set up a question to be displayed on the interactive whiteboard, which students are then able to respond to by using their mobile phones. Questions can be set up so that students can either vote for a specific response, or send longer text answers to the board. When you choose for students to vote (on a scale of one to five, for instance), Poll Everywhere displays a bar chart on the board that updates as students send in their responses, providing a visual way of showing peer assessment.

Poll Everywhere gives two options for students' responses: via a text message or through a phone's web browser. The second of these is always preferable, as it doesn't require students to use their own phone credit for school purposes! Poll Everywhere provides students with a short web address to visit on their mobiles, which presents them with a simple voting box (this page has been carefully designed to work on almost any modern handset).

• As students watch the video of a performance as part of a starter or plenary, ask them to send in responses to the board with their observations. With a trusted class, this could be in the form of a text answer (for example, 'the band stay in time really well'), or it could be in the form of a vote (for example, 'on a scale of one to five, how well do the band stay in time together?'). The responses can then be used as the starting point for a class discussion.

- As a plenary activity at the end of a lesson, ask students to send in a brief message saying what they've achieved during the lesson. These responses can then be loaded up at the start of the next lesson, as a reminder to students and a discussion point.

- After covering a concept, ask students to text in a short summary of what they've learned. As these summaries appear on the board, you can discuss the learning that's taken place and clear up any misunderstandings, making for an effective plenary.

MAKING SPACES AND RESOURCES GO FURTHER

A music department often won't have enough recording equipment to meet demand during certain projects. GCSE classes will usually contain a few guitarists who want to record composition ideas, for example, and juggling resources and spaces to allow for this can be difficult when you have limited recording equipment. The same is also true when these guitarists want to rehearse their performances, requiring amps and practice spaces, which can often be in short supply in a busy department.

There are a growing number of inexpensive adapters (discussed in more detail on page 69) that allow students to plug electric guitars directly into a mobile device such as an iPhone. This allows guitarists to rehearse using headphones (with realistic virtual amps) and to record their composition ideas. A group of guitarists can now rehearse independently (and silently!) in the same classroom, and a lack of recording equipment isn't an issue in supporting their composition. If students have access to smartphones or other handheld devices, a few cheap adapters can be a great investment for a music department.

MOBILE COMPOSITION AND RECORDING

As discussed in the introduction to this chapter, the ability for mobile devices to be used for recording and multitracking is a key benefit to music departments; they can provide an inexpensive and flexible means of extending recording provision for your school.

Crucially, many mobile-phone apps allow for projects to be exported and loaded into computer-based sequencing and notation software (GarageBand for iPad, for instance, allows for work to be exported to a computer in this way). This is a real benefit for music departments, as it allows for students to use devices as virtual notepads for composition ideas, regardless of what instrument they play. Adapters are now becoming available that allow for MIDI keyboards to be plugged into an iPad, iPhone or iPod Touch. These mean that students can record their composition ideas using a keyboard, which they can then import into notation software such as Sibelius.

LEARNING THROUGH MOBILE VIDEO

On page 14 we discussed how online video resources (such as video scores) allow students who can't access traditional notation to make good progress in their music-making. This concept is worth exploring when combined with mobile devices in particular, as it allows students to access these resources entirely on their own terms, stopping and starting as they please while they rehearse different parts.

The majority of smartphones are able to connect to YouTube, giving students access to a vast library of how-to-play videos. This can be useful at GCSE level, where students who are held back by a lack of notation can prepare performances using video scores.

During performance projects with younger students, providing video scores that can be accessed through students' mobile phones is a powerful way of supporting more visual learners in preparing for performances. When students are able to access these resources on their devices, it's essentially like having a virtual teacher sitting next to them. For many students, this means they can make much better progress in developing their instrumental skills and learning new pieces.

MOBILE VIDEO EDITING

When creating video learning resources, editing can make a real difference to the quality of the final output. Mobile editing software (such as iMovie) allows students to film, edit and publish their video to the internet directly from their device. This helps to make the ideas from the 'digital video' chapter on pages 11–28 more feasible, as it cuts out the time-consuming steps involving video cameras, cables, memory cards and transferring files to the computer. It also gives students complete ownership over the videos they create, helping to make the task more engaging and rewarding.

ONLINE RESOURCE

A video guide that demonstrates basic editing with the iMovie mobile app is provided on the book website.
Visit www.rhinegoldeducation.co.uk/dm and use the code ZA6F3W.

SUPPORTING EVERY STUDENT

Mobile devices can have a valuable levelling effect: the music-making tools available on mobiles often aren't reliant on students having had instrumental lessons, which gives every student the opportunity to be musically creative irrespective of their background.

The students in our classrooms have diverse musical tastes and identities. From dubstep to pop, students often have rich musical lives outside of school. The range of sounds and tools that mobile apps offer allow students to explore all of their favourite genres, providing them with sounds that are credible and realistic. This in itself offers a huge boost to engagement; it allows students to align their own musical learning with the artists that they admire and enjoy.

As an example, think of students who are into rapping (or a subgenre such as MCing, spitting or freestyling). Typically, the equipment that a music department owns isn't up to the task of allowing these students to create music in the way that they'd like to, and where schools do have a studio it is often in demand by others who are undertaking courses such as Music Technology. A mobile device with apps such as drum machines, bass-line generators and recording facilities, allow for these students to easily create and record their own music in school.

Whether a student is using their own device or the school's often makes little difference. It may be that students can take the lead in selecting apps and ideas, or this may require some guidance from you. It can be useful to speak to a student about the type of music they'd like to create and work from there, helping them to navigate the myriad of apps that are available to them. This approach can allow previously disinterested students to suddenly become engaged with school music-making.

DJING USING TOUCH DEVICES

One piece of equipment that's maintained its credibility and excitement with students – despite dizzying technological changes happening around it – are the DJ decks. Still in use by the majority of touring popular DJs and dance acts, decks and mixers have remained a staple part of the dance music scene. However, quality decks are expensive, easily damaged and difficult to manage effectively as a resource.

Computer applications that act as virtual decks have been available for quite some time, but mixing is a tactile experience, and when a mouse becomes involved it loses much of its thrill. The larger touch screen of a tablet such as the iPad, however, allows for a perfect mix of software and tactility, allowing virtual decks to finally match the excitement of their physical predecessors.

Crucially, students are able to import their own tracks and music into DJing apps, whether these are beats they've created themselves or tracks from their own listening outside of school. Allowing students to have a creative channel for using their own music to create something new is a great way of engaging harder-to-reach students in music-making.

DJing apps are also much more intuitive than real decks, which are notoriously difficult to use well and require hours of practice. Many apps, for instance, will automatically match the key and tempo of imported tracks, allowing students to start making mixes quickly without the traditional setup requirements. Of course real decks are an instrument in their own right and mastery of them is important for students who wish to expand their DJing skills, but apps provide an engaging first step into the world of mixing for beginners.

When students create their own mixes, it's important to give them an outlet for their work (such as NUMU or YouTube) so their performances can be shared with the rest of the world. Think back to the PS22 Chorus (see pages 23–24), and how sharing their work transformed the experience for the young people involved.

Another way of supporting and celebrating students' DJing creations is to hold a concert in school, for which students can sign up for a DJing slot (a lunchtime concert tends to work well for this as it ensures a good audience). All that needs to be provided is some space, a mobile device and a PA system. Suddenly, students who aren't the usual suspects of the extracurricular scene have an outlet for celebrating their musical creations, which can make a real difference to their engagement with music both in and out of school.

INDEPENDENT GROUP WORK

When students are carrying out group work (especially where there's an element of independent learning involved), progress can often be hindered by forgotten tab sheets, lyrics and other resources. With only one of you and a class full of students, groups can also be left waiting to ask for advice such as how to play a particular chord or how to tune a guitar.

By using a mobile device that's able to access the internet, students can often work much more self-sufficiently in these situations. Lyrics and tabs can be instantly looked up and referred to, and chords can be quickly picked up and used in performance. Guitar tuning apps are also very useful, as they allow guitarists of any level to tune their own instrument.

This approach has the added advantage of freeing up your time; instead of printing chord sheets, tuning guitars and demonstrating chords, you can circulate and spend more time questioning, discussing and supporting students' progress.

In group-work situations, a small number of devices really do go a long way. Just one iPod Touch per group, for instance, can make project work run so much more smoothly. Being self-sufficient is also a crucial skill for students to develop, not only as musicians but also in terms of their more general learning skills.

MANAGING BEHAVIOUR

While mobile devices can offer powerful learning experiences, they're also a source of potential disruption if students don't use them respectfully. But the same is also true of the percussion trolley, keyboards and guitars; music teachers are skilled at managing learning when using potentially disruptive resources. For this reason, music educators are well-placed to manage the responsible use of mobile devices for learning in their classrooms.

The key is to keep the focus on the learning, and to provide students with a clear reason for using a device. If a student has a keyboard in front of them, you would only expect them to use it at the appropriate point in the lesson. Just because students are using the keyboard as part of a learning activity, this doesn't automatically give them the right to play on it whenever they like, and the same is true for mobile devices.

The apprehension that accompanies the prospect of letting students use mobile devices is usually similar to the prospect of opening Pandora's Box, in that once it's been opened it'll be impossible to regain control. Yet any teacher who remembers the dread of first wheeling out the percussion trolley to a class of noisy year 9s during a teaching placement has already been through this experience and survived.

As with all classroom management, it's often a case of intuition. An experienced teacher can tell almost instantly whether a student is using a mobile phone for learning or otherwise after a few moments of observation. For instance if a student is looking withdrawn, phone in hand, while the rest of their group is working, you will usually know that they're not engaged with the task. Fits of giggles emerging from a group of students around a handset, similarly, is a sign that students need to be reminded that they must use the mobile device maturely. Conversely, a student that's playing a guitar and frequently picking up his phone to look at the chord fingerings is clearly engaged in the learning. With a little practice and clear expectations, you can quickly manage the classroom and foster the use of mobiles for learning.

THE TECHNOLOGY

DEVICES

Smartphones are becoming increasingly popular with students as prices continue to drop and the technology becomes more accessible. The iPhone and iPod Touch, which are both popular with students, have access to the App Store: a huge marketplace where mobile apps can be discovered and instantly downloaded, the majority of which are either free or relatively cheap.

Tablet computers, of which the iPad is the most popular, have become one of the fastest selling handheld devices. Offering a larger screen, they allow space for more complex apps to be displayed, and the capabilities of many of these apps are very impressive.

APPS

The various app stores are constantly evolving spaces, with new apps appearing daily. For this reason it isn't possible to provide a comprehensive list of apps here in the book that you might find useful. Having said that, there are a number of key apps that are likely to continue being good choices for the foreseeable future, and these are described below.

A useful exercise can be to ask your students which music-making apps they've come across. This can be helpful not only in discovering apps that might be of use in the classroom, but also in discovering how students are using their mobile devices to make music outside of school.

GARAGEBAND FOR IOS

Like its bigger sibling that runs on the Mac, GarageBand for iOS allows for quick and simple multitrack recording. The iPad and iPhone's built-in microphones can be used for basic recording, and inexpensive add-ons (see page 69) can be used to plug guitars, microphones and even MIDI keyboards into the iPad for recording. The app also offers virtual drums, keyboards and guitars, as well as virtual amplifiers and effects.

Completed songs can be exported by email, allowing students to share their work. Projects can also be exported to GarageBand for Mac, to be enhanced further using a desktop computer.

FL STUDIO MOBILE

Offering credible sounds for dance-music creation, this app allows students to build up compositions using loops, drums and sequencers directly on their mobile devices. It's especially engaging for students who enjoy rap or dance music, and they find that they're quickly able to build up backing tracks and dance pieces using the intuitive interface. Many such students already use FL studio at home (the bigger sibling for the computer), and this mobile version allows them to bring their knowledge from home into the classroom.

MY NOTE GAMES

This app allows students to practise and get feedback on their notation and instrumental skills. Students are guided through a series of notation-based lessons and tasks; as they play their instrument, the iPhone detects the pitches they're playing and scores them based on how accurately they've performed. What makes it particularly versatile is that it can be used with any instrument, from the violin to the recorder, and the instant feedback is appreciated by students.

MADPAD

MadPad is a mixing application that incorporates video in an innovative way. Short video clips are recorded using the camera on a mobile device; typically each clip contains something that produces a tone or rhythm. After a number of these clips have been recorded, they're presented in a grid on the screen, and by activating each clip using the touch screen a composition can be created. This app works well when exploring the musical possibilities of found sounds (such as percussive noises like rattling keys or closing doors). It's also a fun class activity when students are split into small groups and asked to create their own loops (using body percussion for instance), which are then recorded and mixed together.

STUDIOMINI

StudioMini replicates a simple four-track recorder, allowing students to build up compositions without the need for a computer or any other recording equipment. It has a surprising number of features for a mobile app, and options such as pre-recorded drum backings and a guitar-chord bank are useful in allowing students to be self-sufficient when recording and experimenting.

DJAY

As its name suggests, djay is an app that replicates the functions of DJ decks, allowing students to remix tracks in an intuitive and accessible way. Sound files can be imported for use in mixes, allowing students to use songs that are suited to their tastes.

PIANO*

Piano* is a tuition app that aims to teach simple keyboard skills, using on-screen lessons on a coloured keyboard. Of course, an app is no match for an instrumental teacher, but it can present an engaging first step for students who would like to learn basic keyboard skills. The interface is impressive, and incorporates traditional notation while remaining engaging and intuitive.

ONLINE RESOURCE

A video guide that covers and reviews further apps is provided on the book website.

PERIPHERALS

Add-ons for mobile devices (particularly iPads, iPhones and iPods) have become a big business in recent years, and peripherals that expand their music-making capabilities are beginning to emerge.

IRIG

This is a guitar adapter for iPad, iPhone and iPod Touch that allows for electric guitars to be plugged directly into the device for recording, rehearsal and performance. The sound quality is surprisingly good and it can be used with any music-making app, from GarageBand to the many guitar amp simulators in the App Store. The iRig comes into its own when used with students' own devices, as it allows for them to rehearse and record their ideas in any space, using headphones.

IRIG MIC

This is a condenser microphone that plugs directly into mobile devices, offering impressive sound quality when recording student performances straight to the device. Like the iRig, it's compatible with any app that allows audio input, so students can use it to build up compositions in a mobile sequencer (alongside built-in loops and synthesisers).

MIDI INPUTS

Accessories that allow MIDI devices to be used with mobile devices are starting to emerge, meaning that students can control synthesisers, notate their work and add to compositions in a more traditional manner. Previously, this has squarely been the domain of the PCs sitting around the music classroom with MIDI keyboards attached, and it's exciting to see this approach is becoming more mobile.

 CASE STUDY

BEN SMITH, TRAFALGAR SCHOOL, VICTORIA, AUSTRALIA

Ben Smith regularly uses a small set of six school-owned iPads in his music lessons, alongside students' own devices such as iPods. As part of an approach to learning in a Musical Futures manner, Ben describes how mobile devices allow students to access the resources they need to make progress:

'I encourage the students to bring iPods to class, especially their iPod Touches, as I can hook them up to the school wireless network to give them instant and portable access to a variety of media for learning in class. The students like having access to their own music when working in groups, learning songs or learning instrumental parts, and having easy access to the internet and YouTube has proven to make learning quicker, more efficient, personalised and portable.'

The key to making effective use of students' own devices is the ability to connect them to the school's wireless internet network. When Ben initially started working with the devices, he needed to liaise with his school technician to ensure the necessary access was in place for students. 'The only difficulties I came up against was connecting to the network, as our school was initially not set up to handle them, but this was quickly resolved through a discussion with our IT Tech.'

Alongside instant access to musical resources and media, the devices in Ben's classroom are also used by students in a more traditional way. When rehearsing a performance of a popular song that required a number of xylophones, a group of students found that the old xylophones in the cupboard weren't up to the task as they were out of tune due to humidity damage.

The problem was smoothly solved by a student, who asked if there were any xylophone apps for the iPad, 'because that would be easier to play'. 'A few moments later,' Ben recounts, 'we were installing xylophone apps on the six iPads and created a very successful iPad ensemble. The class absolutely nailed the song and the virtual xylophones sounded great! The beauty of the iPad app was that we had access to a variety of xylophones, glockenspiels and marimbas all within one app, providing the ensemble with a variety of sounds to play with.

'The benefits are wide and varied. If students have instant access to knowledge, ideas, creativity, resources and communication all on one small and easy-to-carry device, how can that be a bad thing? Schools never have enough money to provide computers to all students in every classroom, but with the introduction of mobile devices more students have more access more often.

'We use iPod Touches that the students bring with them for photography classes, multimedia lessons, internet access and many great apps that assist with learning, not to mention developing creativity skills. Compared to laptops, mobile devices such as the iPod Touch and iPad are fairly cheap and very easy to use, and can provide a number of services through apps that laptops can't, without spending hundreds of dollars on software. For example, GarageBand on the iPod or iPad is very cheap but if you want a similar piece of software for a laptop you can spend much more, and this makes the iPad or iPod a great solution! The students love using them. They can use them for learning anywhere, anytime, and can use them comfortably without carrying power supplies and cables with them.'

Ben goes on to explain further the benefits for music learning that he's seen as a result of his iPads. 'In my classroom they have helped develop the musical skills of my students through the use of virtual instruments, access to apps that develop music theory, YouTube, and internet access on the spot, especially as part of group projects. It also helps that it's a product the students know and love, and can use intuitively.'

Ben sees great value in accessing the tools that students are using outside of school for learning, and is often surprised by the ingenuity with which students make use of these devices. 'At a concert last year, one of my students used an iPod Touch as a guitar amp, using an app called AmpliTube and an iRig guitar adapter. This mobile technology is engaging, enthralling and easy to use, and if the kids can use it so successfully outside of school, we should be using it inside school. In the right hands, and with the right teacher guidance, they can help make learning easier and a lot more engaging.'

The use of an iPad has also made a difference to Ben's life as a music teacher, and he's found that he uses his laptop less and less as the iPad has become a vital part of his daily teaching practice. 'Yes, there are things a laptop can do that an iPad can't, but for day-to-day teaching, creative apps and online web tools, the iPad wins easily. The only thing I use my laptop for now is burning a DVD after doing video editing (although I can now do editing on the iPad too); everything else is done on the iPad.

'It's portable and light to hold and carry, the battery lasts up to 10 hours on one charge, it's easy to use, easy to look at, there are tonnes of apps that can allow you to pretty much do anything you want to do, not to mention access the internet wherever you are. You can connect it to TVs, projectors, PA systems, guitar amps, cameras, you can film with it, take photos and then edit them all and post to the web or transfer to a computer for later.'

(Email interview with Ben Smith, January 2012)

VIRTUAL LEARNING ENVIRONMENTS

In recent years, the Virtual Learning Environment (or VLE) has become a permanent fixture in schools across the country. Although almost all schools have one, the extent to which they are used varies, from those where the VLE is central to everyday life to schools where it's there in the background but isn't given much attention. What's common among teachers in most schools, though, is that niggling feeling that they ought to be making more use of it than they are. It's similar to having an underused gym membership: you know that it's there and you know that you'll benefit if you go regularly, but long, busy days at school have a habit of getting in the way of good intentions!

Throughout this book, we've started to explore the huge selection of online and digital-media resources that are valuable to a music teacher. A key issue is how to share and make these resources available to students in a way that's safe and convenient. You might have created the world's best Spotify playlist, podcast or revision video, but if students aren't able to find it quickly when they need it, this presents a barrier to the learning. In many cases, the VLE is the natural place to pull these resources together, allowing you to create an engaging and interactive learning hub for your students.

A common way of using the VLE is simply to upload a few PowerPoint files and Word documents from lessons. While this approach is certainly better than not putting any materials online at all, it doesn't allow you to use the VLE to its full potential.

Imagine, for a moment, that you're a 15-year-old GCSE music student. You live in a world of Xbox, YouTube, Facebook and instant messaging. How likely is it that you're going to be motivated to spend time in the evening reading through PowerPoint files from a lesson on the VLE? How much more likely is it that you'd be willing to log on to watch a video from today's lesson of your friends explaining key concepts, and then contribute to a discussion forum, summing up what you learnt during the lesson?

Like any resource, the VLE is most powerful when it's thoughtfully integrated into classroom practice and woven into schemes of work or projects. Alongside VLEs often comes the phrase 'extending learning beyond the classroom'. This is only possible if some thought has been put into exactly *how* the learning is going to be extended, and this chapter presents some ideas for ensuring VLE usage is meaningful and focused.

Although the VLE is primarily a learning tool, it also has the potential to free up your time and to make a music department run more smoothly. This impacts on the learning indirectly, as it allows for music staff to focus more time on doing what's important: teaching music. Alongside the learning ideas, this chapter also discusses ways in which you can start to free up your time in this way.

It's worth noting that many of the ideas contained in this chapter will work just as well using a blog, and the reverse is also true of the 'blogs' chapter on pages 85–94 (which also covers some of the privacy issues that need to be tackled when using a blog in place of a VLE). As discussed in the introduction, cross-over is to be expected when working with internet-based resources; there are so many ways to achieve the same outcome using different tools. The key is for you to pick the ideas and technologies that suit you and your students best.

There's a large variety of VLE products on the market, so this chapter doesn't go into the specifics of how to achieve tasks on different platforms (online video guides haven't been provided to accompany this chapter for the same reason). However, although VLEs are all slightly different, there's always a common set of core items on the menu; whichever VLE your school uses, you'll be able to try out the ideas presented in this chapter.

Because many schools view the VLE as an important resource, you should be able to access in-house training, help and support in getting started and implementing your ideas. If this help is available to you, it's well worth seeking it out and taking advantage of it.

CREATING AN ENGAGING HUB

You recognise good learning when you see it and you know what makes a good music lesson. Engagement, interaction, variety and the excitement of music-making are all key features of effective and enjoyable musical learning. However, this doesn't only apply to the classroom. Learning is learning, whether it's taking place in a classroom, a practice room or online. The same thought that goes into the planning of a great lesson also needs to go into the planning of a great online learning space, and the aim of this chapter is to show you how to create an engaging online learning hub, quickly and easily, using a VLE.

SETTING UP LEARNING SPACES

First, you'll need to decide how you'd like your spaces in the VLE to be organised. This depends on how you work as a department and how your learning is structured. In many cases, a simple structure with a space for each year group will work well, with different sections within each year group for the various projects or units of work that students undertake.

It can be tempting to begin by creating a vast structure of spaces, but it's definitely best to take it steady. Pick one class or year group, create a space for them, and work on integrating it into your lessons. Once you're confident, you can then move forward with creating further spaces. It's much better to slowly build up a collection of populated and well thought out online spaces than to have a vast network of empty ones.

EMBEDDING LEARNING CONTENT

Embedding is a feature that's cropping up more and more across the internet. It's essentially the action of creating a small window on a web (or VLE) page, through which a piece of content from another website is displayed. When sites allow their content to be embedded, they provide a short piece of code that tells your VLE how big the window should be and where it should link to. YouTube, for example, allows for its videos to be embedded in any other site, and provides an embed code underneath each video for this purpose.

Crucially, this allows for all sorts of exciting online content to be drawn together into a VLE page, from videos and audio to interactive composition tools. Many of the tools that have been explored elsewhere in this book are capable of being embedded into a VLE, and at this point it's worth recapping a few that are of particular use in creating an engaging VLE space, along with some practical ideas for how they can be used to enhance the learning.

CLASSROOM IDEA

ONLINE VIDEO

YouTube, along with other major video-sharing sites, allows for the vast majority of their videos to be embedded. This opens up an entire world of learning content that can be pulled directly through to pages on your VLE, providing students with a highly visual and engaging means of learning.

- Create a page for a specific performance project, and upload resources that allow students to continue making progress at home. Video scores (either created by you or sourced from YouTube) can be provided alongside lyric sheets and scores, allowing students to learn in the way that best suits them. This encourages students to learn independently, selecting the resources that they find most useful (whether it's a score, tab sheet or video). This is a particularly useful method for teachers who are undertaking the Musical Futures approach.

- YouTube is also awash with performances and cover versions of songs that musicians from across the world have uploaded. Within a VLE page it's possible to embed these side by side, allowing students to compare and contrast the performances, and gain inspiration for their own compositions and arrangements. Adding a simple vote, survey or discussion forum (see pages 80–81) is a great way of focusing their thoughts and allowing them to interact with the content you've embedded.

- YouTube also contains thousands of videos that explain specific musical and instrumental techniques, such as the circle of 5ths or violin harmonics. Embedding these videos into a VLE allows you to carefully curate a set of engaging video resources that students can use to learn independently.

CLASSROOM IDEA

ONLINE AUDIO

Any tracks that have been uploaded to NUMU can easily be embedded into a VLE. This allows for students' own work from lessons to be pulled through to a space on your VLE, which helps to give the students ownership of the learning space you've created. Regularly uploading content from lessons is the best way to ensure that students visit their VLE space frequently.

Embedding audio in this way, combined with a simple VLE voting tool, is a great way of implementing the competition idea from pages 30–32.

NUMU also offers an embeddable widget that automatically pulls through the latest tracks uploaded to a school's NUMU space. This is helpful in ensuring that your VLE space is regularly updated with little effort on your part. It's also possible to embed this on the school's main website, which is a great way of highlighting the music-making happening across the school to a wider community.

Although it's often possible to upload audio directly to a VLE, it's usually preferable to use the embedding approach (via NUMU) as it kills two birds with one stone: it makes the music available to a wider audience, at the same time as neatly pulling it through to the more private VLE space. This combination of public and private sharing is a real engagement booster for students: suddenly the work from their music lessons has a global audience, as well as being featured in a private space where more focused, teacher-led learning can happen.

ONLINE WEB TOOLS

Many small interactive music tools (such as iNudge, mentioned on pages 95–96) can be directly embedded into a VLE page. This gives students an opportunity to create music from your VLE space, allowing them to interact with the page each time they visit.

CLASSROOM IDEA

ORGANISE A BUSY DEPARTMENT

With numerous peripatetic lessons, rehearsals and concerts taking place in addition to classroom teaching, music departments are typically the busiest in the school. You will be well aware of the thought and effort that's needed to keep a department running smoothly, and often a department noticeboard is the main point of call for students and visiting teachers.

However, the humble department noticeboard does have its limitations, the main one being that it can only be viewed (and added to) by somebody standing in front of it. This means that parents aren't able to look at it regularly, and that visiting teachers can only update it while they're in school.

A VLE solution, on the other hand, has none of these limitations. Students and parents are able to access it from home, meaning fewer missed lessons due to forgotten lesson times or misplaced instruments. On most VLEs, it's possible to give visiting teachers the ability to edit and update schedules from home.

Having an online departmental calendar that's constantly updated is also a good way of using a VLE to help keep things running smoothly. Most VLEs allow for multiple calendars to be created, and this can be a particularly useful feature as it allows you to create different calendars for different audiences. For example, you could create one calendar that only shows events relevant to parents. Another calendar could be created for peripatetic teachers, providing them with a single port of call for arranging rehearsals and booking rooms.

CLASSROOM IDEA

COORDINATE SCHOOL PRODUCTIONS

School productions, while being one of the most rewarding aspects of the job for many teachers, are also one of the most stressful. Coordinating musicians, actors, set designers, sound mixers and lighting operators through a busy timetable of rehearsals can be a daunting task.

By creating an online space that's a one-stop shop for all of those involved in a production, you can use it to coordinate all of the performers, rehearsals and tasks, helping things to run more smoothly and reducing some of the stress for the teachers involved.

The following tips will help you to create an online space that keeps things in check when it's school-production season:

- Add a clear rehearsal schedule, and make sure everyone knows that this is the definitive version they need to refer to. This makes it easier for teachers to update, without having to maintain a number of schedules posted on different notice boards.

- Add any resources that performers might need, such as scripts, lyric sheets and audio recordings that will help them in their preparation. This also helps to ensure that students turn up to rehearsals with everything they need.

- As the rehearsals progress, the ideas on pages 12–13 can be adapted to help students measure their progress leading towards the final performance. Uploading an MP3 recording or video performance from a rehearsal (having checked with the publisher that this is acceptable under their copyright terms), along with a little feedback and details of what students need to practise before the next rehearsal, can be a great way of ensuring focused progress and getting the best from performers.

- A countdown that shows the number of weeks to the final performance can be a good reminder for students (and staff). This can be manually updated weekly, but for the more technically minded there are a number of free, automatic countdown timers on the internet that can be embedded into a VLE page.

 CLASSROOM IDEA

COVER WORK

With a lot of coursework and content to get through, you may often be left feeling anxious that students will slip behind when you can't make it into school. Rather than relying on the member of staff covering the lesson to relay work to your students, you could use the VLE to leave personal messages for your students, outlining exactly what they're expected to work on during the lesson.

The brave could even leave a video message for students, allowing you to be there virtually to introduce the lesson and explain to students what they're to do during the time available. By combining this approach with the ideas from the 'digital video' chapter on pages 11–28, you could also provide video learning materials (such as a video score) for students to make use of during the lesson.

In addition, you could upload a bank of cover-lesson resources to your VLE that colleagues and cover staff could use in the case of unexpected absence, allowing you to provide students with meaningful activities to complete. This works best when it's a collaborative effort, with teachers from across a department uploading cover ideas that relate to specific topics or year groups. Over time, this can become a valuable and comprehensive resource for such situations.

Your cover-lesson bank could contain, for example:

- Printable sheets that can be used by cover staff as a basis for lessons.

- Listening activities with links to online resources such as YouTube videos. When combined with the quiz tools that most VLEs feature, this can be a great way of allowing cover teachers to lead discussions and assess students' knowledge.

- Step-by-step mini projects that are designed to last for a single lesson, which non-specialist teachers can confidently lead, complete with any required resources that can be immediately downloaded or played.

- Embedded web tools (such as those covered on pages 95–99); these can be very helpful for cover lessons, as they're intuitive to use and allow students to create music from within a web browser. If a computer room is available, this can form a self-contained activity that requires no external resources.

 CLASSROOM IDEA

DISCUSSION FORUMS

Online learning is so much more engaging when students are able to contribute themselves. All VLEs have a function that allows for students to contribute safely to discussions, and this can be a great way of allowing students to demonstrate and discuss their learning. The ability to communicate effectively and respectfully online is becoming an important life and career skill, and discussion forums are a key way in which knowledge is shared and developed online.

- Add a discussion forum to the class page of an examination group (GCSE for instance), which students can use to raise any issues or questions that they have during the course. As well as your input, students should also be encouraged to help each other out, which allows them to demonstrate their knowledge by explaining concepts to others. If a student requests help, you could even ask another student who you know has grasped the concept to explain it on the discussion forum.

- Create a discussion forum that allows students to have an input into the topics, styles and pieces studied at points throughout the year. This works especially well where class performances are used as part of a Musical Futures approach, as students can discuss the pieces they'd like to perform (with musical justifications to support their suggestions). Allowing students to have a voice in this way can help to increase their engagement.

TIPS FOR DISCUSSION FORUMS

You'll need to browse the forum regularly, just to check that everything is ticking along nicely. In the classroom, the teacher's voice is an important part of the learning and it's the same online. Your contributions, questions and observations will be welcomed by students, and will help to keep the conversation flowing. It's usually possible for you to set up an email alert that lets you know when new submissions have been added, making it easier to keep track of them and to know when students have requested help.

If any behaviour issues do crop up, deal with them quickly and robustly. If swearing or bullying takes place in a school discussion forum, for instance, it should be treated in the same way as it would if it happened in a lesson. Many schools that use discussion forums find that any initial issues quickly subside if they're dealt with swiftly in the first instance.

 CLASSROOM IDEA

SURVEYS AND QUIZZES

These are a quick and easy feature to use in a VLE space. They allow students to demonstrate their knowledge in slightly different ways: both present a series of questions, but while the quiz gives immediate feedback, the survey simply allows students to vote on a topic or send a response for you to mark.

- At the end of a unit of work or as a homework task, ask students to complete a simple multiple-choice quiz that runs through some of the key musical terms which have been covered.

- Alongside a piece of audio that contains some unidentified cadences, add a quiz that lets students guess the cadence. This is an effective and engaging task, and quick for you to create when armed with an MP3 recorder and a piano (see pages 36–37).

• Before a revision session, use a survey to allow students to vote on the content that they'd most like to be covered.

CLASSROOM IDEA

INTEGRATE YOUR SCHEMES OF WORK

For a VLE to make a significant impact on students' learning, it must be woven into what's happening in the classroom. Rather than being an add-on, it should be seen as an integral part of teaching and learning. The best way of doing this is to ensure that schemes of work and departmental plans give teachers clear opportunities to extend learning using online tools and the VLE.

A good place to start is by sitting down with one unit of work or project and deciding if there are any natural opportunities to integrate online tools in a meaningful way. As VLEs are typically accessed by students at home, homework is a natural place to start integrating the VLE into a scheme of work. Setting students specific homework that works in conjunction with digital media can be a valuable way of extending their learning. Ideas from across the book are well-suited to this, but as a reminder here are a few key homework ideas:

• Embed video footage of a class performance, and ask students to contribute in some way (for example by leaving a detailed comment in a discussion forum).

• Add a listening task, either by embedding a YouTube clip or linking to a Spotify track, and ask students to leave a comment that answers a specific homework question related to the track.

• At the end of a lesson or topic, assign each student a key term and ask them to add their own explanation of it to the VLE.

• Upload students' compositions as embedded audio files and ask students to leave comments outlining what they like about each one, along with some possible areas for development (using musical terminology and justifications).

The idea of flipping the classroom from page 16 (where learning content is presented online for students to cover before a lesson) is also an interesting way of using a VLE. It allows students to learn content in their own time and then apply this knowledge in lessons. The case study on pages 92–94 outlines how a music department has found this approach very successful.

TIPS FOR VLE USE

It's worth reiterating: do make use of any help, support and training that's available to you at your school. If you need some training or you're not sure how to use a certain function, approach your school technicians – they will usually be able to point you in the right direction. The online resources that accompany this chapter on the book website will also help to get you started.

For departments that decide to use their VLE to help organise matters, it's important to switch exclusively to the online system from day one. Although it may seem like a good idea to maintain a paper system while making the transition, this often leads to people simply ignoring the online version and continuing as they've always done. A decisive and well-publicised switch to the VLE version is the best way to ensure that the change sticks and brings about a reduced workload for your department.

BLOGS

The blog is another one of those mysterious terms that actually represents a fairly simple idea. The word itself is derived from the phrase 'web log', and a blog takes the form of an online diary that users can easily update on a regular basis. These updates are called posts, and they're presented on the blog in chronological order, with the newest at the top. Blog posts can contain digital media such as audio, video and photos, and usually visitors are able to leave comments on the posts.

The technology behind blogging is fairly simple: it's basically just a web page. However the *concept* of blogging is powerful, and the blog format has quickly become a prominent mode of online expression.

The ease with which blogs can be set up and updated is one of the main reasons for their popularity. At the time when blogs emerged, creating and maintaining a website was a laborious and technically difficult task. Then blogs came along and a few clicks later, everyone had an accessible way to add their voice to the internet. You might have heard of the term 'Web 2.0': this marked the point at which people started *adding* content to the web, as opposed to merely consuming it, and it was blogging that really started this trend. Sites like Facebook and Twitter are both an evolution of the blogging concept.

In the world of music, blogging has become an important channel for musicians to communicate with their fans. Orchestras, pop celebrities and new talent are all using blogs to communicate and promote their work. Crucially, blogs allow musicians to express their own personalities and interact with fans directly (although in the case of pop celebrities, it's often their PR firms doing the blogging on their behalf!).

The ease with which blogs can be set up and kept updated makes them a versatile tool for supporting musical learning. The ideas in this chapter detail some of the ways in which you can make use of blogs to support students' learning. The 'professional development' chapter on page 107 discusses blogging as a means of developing your professional practice and discovering new ideas.

Many VLEs also offer the ability to create blogs, and it's worth mentioning again that the ideas presented in this chapter will often work just as well on a VLE.

TEACHER BLOGS FOR STUDENTS

Because of its diary-like nature, a blog can be an ideal way for you to create a regularly updated space for a particular group of students. You could use this space to:

• Chart students' progress from week to week

• Present audio and video footage from lessons

• Provide feedback and encouragement

• Present interesting content to expand students' musical learning.

Tumblr (described in more detail on page 91) is a great platform for creating this type of blog, as it allows for video, audio and photos to be quickly added to blog posts, and it also allows for password protection of a blog.

 CLASSROOM IDEA

TEACHER CLASS UPDATES

Writing learning aims and objectives on the whiteboard at the start of each lesson has become part of most teachers' practice, but once the lesson is over and the aims are wiped off the board, they can be easily forgotten by students. As music is largely a practical subject, students often won't have exercise books to remind them of what's been covered previously as they would in other subjects. A class blog, updated by you each week, can be a great way of documenting students' learning and signposting the learning journey.

1. Set up a blog for a particular class, and distribute the address to your students (either by giving them the blog address during a lesson, or by linking to it from an area of your VLE).

2. After each lesson, spend a few minutes updating the blog with a brief commentary on how the lesson went.

3. Refer to the learning objectives, the activities that students took part in, and how well they met the learning objectives.

4. Be sure to give praise to students and groups, and use the blog to celebrate their achievements – along with providing pointers for improvement during the next lesson. If you do want to name students individually, it's best to create a private, secure blog within your VLE.

5. At the beginning of each lesson, load up the blog for a quick reminder of what was achieved during the previous lesson.

CLASSROOM IDEA

WIDER LISTENING

At GCSE and A level, encouraging students to listen to a wide range of music can help them to develop their listening skills and musical knowledge. A blog can be a perfect way of supporting students in this endeavour, as it allows for listening to be curated and signposted by the teacher on a regular basis.

1. Create a 'wider listening' blog, and set the expectation in lessons that as part of their ongoing coursework, students should listen to at least one piece per week/fortnight.

2. Regularly update the blog with Spotify or YouTube links, which allow your students to access a piece with a single click (the easier you make this for students, the more likely it is that they'll listen to the music!)

3. To further encourage your students, add a very brief commentary to each blog post that accompanies the link, setting the scene for the piece and highlighting anything that students should listen out for. A brief blog post of this kind might look like this:

Charles Ives – The Alcotts (insert Spotify link here)

Charles Ives was an American modernist composer, and this movement is from one of his most famous works: Piano Sonata No. 2 (1920). Listen out for his use of dissonance, and how it's used to create contrast and tension.

The aim here is to encourage students to enjoy listening to a wide range of music, and be excited by listening to new works, so it's important not to make this activity feel like 'work' as such. Posts should be brief, interesting and varied.

CLASSROOM IDEA

STUDENT PROGRESS BLOGGING

Blogs don't have to be maintained just by you; asking students to update their own blogs can be equally valuable. Blogs can give students a quick and easy way to track and reflect on their own progress; the ability for you and other students to comment on their posts can make this all the more worthwhile.

The aim here is for students to not only blog about their learning, but to also reflect on it and consider the progress they're making, and how they can improve. Because each blog is personal to a particular student, they often have a sense of real ownership over their spaces, fostering a feeling of pride in their musical achievements which can, in turn, impact on their progress during lessons.

• To start with, each student will need a blog. They could create one using one of the sites discussed later in the chapter (see pages 90–92), but if your VLE has the ability to create blogs for groups of students then this will probably help you to keep track of them more easily.

• At the end of each lesson or as a homework task, ask students to create a blog post about the progress they've made during the lesson and what they've learned. At first some teacher guidance will be useful here; it's important to stress that the aim is to be reflective, rather than to simply list facts or achievements from the lesson. Giving students a few phrases to start them off can be helpful, such as: 'Today I was most proud of...', or 'Next week, the thing I need to work on most is...'.

• If you have easy access to computers (or mobile devices) then this can make a great plenary activity, but it may work better as a homework task as students will be able to spend more time on their entries.

• Encouraging students to comment on each other's blogs (in a supportive way) can be valuable. Again, it's useful to give students some guidance on the type of comments they could make, to help keep the focus on the learning.

• It's worth trying this idea with a smaller group first, so you can get to grips with keeping track of students' blogs before rolling it out to a larger group. That said, checking students' blogs isn't too much of a chore and can often be quite interesting.

• For a twist on this idea (and where time is limited), it can be interesting to restrict students to short Twitter-style updates (of no more than 140 characters, which is similar to the size of a standard text message).

Student blogs can be easily adapted depending on different tasks and projects. With group work, for instance, it can be useful to have a collaborative blog that students take turns in updating on behalf of the group. As time passes, students' progress blogs quickly become an important part of their learning, allowing them to chart and celebrate their progress throughout their musical development.

CLASSROOM IDEA

INSTRUMENTAL PRACTICE DIARIES

The idea of students' blogging about their progress can be especially useful when it comes to instrumental lessons. Dog-eared practice diaries are commonplace in music departments, but all too often their use quickly diminishes as the weeks pass, and they're not always used to their full potential. By asking students to blog instead, it can bring the idea of a practice diary to life. These blogs also give you a useful overview of students' instrumental progress, which can be helpful at GCSE when students are preparing for exam performances alongside their classroom work.

1. Students will need a blog each for this idea. If your VLE has a blogging function this can be useful, as it will probably have built-in features that allow you to manage and supervise the content of multiple student blogs more easily than a service such as Tumblr.

2. Ask students to fill in the blog each week, detailing how long they've practised for, what their targets are and what they've achieved. It can help to provide students with a template to guide them in the right direction and get them started.

3. For students who are comfortable with it, video footage from instrumental lessons, performances and practice sessions can also be uploaded, helping to create a rich record of their musical learning and development.

4. Encourage parents to visit the blog. Commenting allows parents to contribute to students' diaries in a meaningful way; adding their voice to the learning conversation can be a great way of engaging them in their students' musical learning.

CLASSROOM IDEA

VIDEO BLOGS

A video blog (or vlog) is simply a blog in video format, with new videos being regularly uploaded and presented chronologically. This can work well when combined with the ideas from the 'digital video' chapter, such as in cases where you want to upload regular videos to chart students' progress. Tumblr is the easiest way of presenting a video blog, as it means videos can be instantly uploaded without any fuss, and also allows for password protection of a blog.

1. Create a blog for a particular class, distributing the web address and password to your students.

2. Each week, upload a few progress videos of the class. Add your voice to the blog by leaving some short comments on the progress that has been made, along with an indication of what needs to be worked on next week. If students have already watched the videos as part of a plenary and discussed their progress, their own feedback can be summarised on the blog by you.

3. At the end of a particular project, it can be useful to post a final video alongside a link to the first video you uploaded. This before-and-after demonstration allows students to see clearly the progress they've made.

4. If you're comfortable with students commenting on the blog, this can be a great thing to encourage. On pages 12–13 we discussed how important it is to set clear expectations and routines for student assessment, and this is vital when it comes to leaving comments, as students will usually be doing so away from the classroom.

PODCAST BLOGS

For a podcast to truly be a podcast, it needs to be posted online in a way that makes it easy to download regularly. A blog can provide a great way of doing this. Tumblr is an easy platform through which to share audio as it has a built-in tool that allows for audio files to be uploaded in a few clicks. Students are then able to listen to the podcast online via the web page, or download it as an audio file to be added to their own mobile device or MP3 player. It's also easy for them to look back through previous podcasts to find the content they need when it comes to revision time. To aid this, it's worth adding a few bullet points of text to each podcast that provides your students with a brief outline of what it contains.

THE TECHNOLOGY

Blogging has evolved rapidly and there are a wide range of blogging platforms that you can make use of, each with their own features and quirks. Despite this rapid evolution, there are a number of platforms that have stood the test of time, which offer functions that you are likely to find useful. Some of these are described below.

All of the services mentioned here have apps that can be used to upload content to a blog from a mobile device, making it easier for you to keep them current and updated. Some even allow for video and audio to be posted directly from a mobile device, which can be great for uploading student work during a lesson.

TUMBLR (www.tumblr.com)

You are likely to find Tumblr a good choice as it's one of the simplest platforms to use, it looks great, and it's been designed to incorporate rich media such as audio, video and photos.

A Tumblr blog can be created with ease and once you have chosen a name for your blog, it sits at an address that can be given to students or linked to from a VLE (for example, y11music.tumblr.com).

Different themes can be applied to a Tumblr blog that allow you to customise how it looks, and a unique visual presentation can add credibility in the eyes of your students. Blogs can also be password protected and by distributing this password to students, you can create a space that's not visible on the wider internet.

One of the best features of Tumblr is that it allows short videos, audio files and photos to be directly uploaded to a blog post, without having to upload them elsewhere and use embed codes to pull them through.

ONLINE RESOURCE

A video guide to setting up a blog with Tumblr (including how to upload media) is provided on the book website.
Visit www.rhinegoldeducation.co.uk/dm and use the code ZA6F3W.

POSTEROUS (http://posterous.com)

Posterous is similar to Tumblr in that it allows you to upload various types of media, and it also offers password protection. It provides more features than Tumblr so the more technically minded may find it useful, but it also requires a little more effort than Tumblr to get up and running with.

WORDPRESS (http://wordpress.com)

Again for the more technically minded, WordPress offers far more options for customisation than Tumblr. It's a powerful platform that's now being used to create full websites, with thousands of plug-ins and themes available (although many at a price) that allow users to shape the look and feel of their blogs to suit their needs.

Although Tumblr is probably the most suitable option if you want a simple way of sharing content with students, WordPress is great if you have more technical skills and would like to put these to use in customising your site.

EDUBLOGS (http://edublogs.com)

Although there is a small cost, this is a useful service if you would like to create and oversee a number of individual student blogs. The service has been designed exclusively for school use, so its features should be well-suited to your needs.

The main benefit of Edublogs over the others mentioned above is that you can create a set of blogs for an entire class, and have full control and oversight of their spaces. This is useful if you would like students to have individual blogs, but aren't able to create them through your school's VLE.

 CASE STUDY

DANNY FISHER, HEAD OF MUSIC TECHNOLOGY, SIMON BALLE SCHOOL, HERTFORDSHIRE

Danny Fisher uses blogs and online video to provide learning materials for his own students, but has also found that his resources have gained attention from a much wider audience. Along with the use of video resources and mobile devices, the blog has made a huge impact on students' musical learning across the school.

The department has a number of blogs, including a main department blog that acts as a prospectus and a portal to other content (www.simonballemusic.info). This blog also has a Google Calendar embedded within it, showing upcoming rehearsals and events. The blog element of this page is used to publicise events and celebrate students' musical achievements; it often features video and audio content of performances and school events.

This multimedia content is also a feature of the Music Technology blog (http://sbsmusictech.wordpress.com), which is populated with large amounts of learning materials to accompany the A-level course. Homework is set through the blog, course documents and exemplar work from previous years are provided, and all of the content is presented in a slick and well-organised way.

It's important for online learning spaces to promote interactivity, and the department uses online surveys and forms to allow students to demonstrate their learning. Crucially, these spaces aren't just an afterthought: they're integrated into schemes of work and projects, and are a key feature of students' learning. They're often part of a flipped-classroom model (see page 16), where students learn material using the online resources and then complete a quiz to show what they've understood, the results of which inform the teacher's planning of the following lesson. This gives teachers the time and information they need to support effectively students' learning, and acts as an early warning system to indicate when students have struggled with a concept.

It's not just the teachers who create content for the blog: students also create their own video content as part of their Music Technology lessons. These video resources, which explain topics such as how to use the school studio or different types of microphone, have a number of benefits to students' learning. They allow students to consolidate and demonstrate what they've learned in a way that they find engaging. The fact that the videos are shared publicly and used by others also gives them a sense of credibility and value, which motivates students to ensure that they're high quality. Students also find them useful when it comes to revision time.

Danny explains that when a student gets stuck on how to use the studio, or needs some advice on a particular piece of equipment, they don't need to wait to find a teacher; they can simply visit the blog and search for the information they need to know. The fact that students can also read the blog on their smartphones means that they're able to access these videos wherever they are, without having to find a computer, and a mature attitude towards the use of mobile devices for learning has been fostered by the department.

Lower down in the school, blogs are also used as part of KS3 Musical Futures projects, where video and audio recordings are used to share and celebrate students' performances. The blogs also play a part in students' learning when preparing for performances, and again the ability to stream video to students' mobile phones is a key aspect of this. Danny explains that 'we became increasingly aware of how many students are learning outside of school using YouTube tutorials. It's something that kids are doing already anyway, so we decided to bring this into the classroom.'

Students now regularly access video tutorials on their mobile devices, and for some students this has been a breakthrough. Danny describes a situation that many music teachers will be familiar with: some students just learn best when the teacher is sitting next to them demonstrating how to play or do something. This can lead to frustration for the music teacher, who'd like to be able to support many students in this way but can sadly only be in one place at a time. By creating video resources that can be accessed on students' mobiles, however, Danny has effectively been able to multiply himself, being virtually available to students on demand.

At Simon Balle, classroom music teachers aren't the only ones blogging: the visiting instrumental staff also find blogs useful in organising their timetables and communicating with students and parents. Instrumental teachers also upload learning content for students to access from home, and their use of blogs for both organisation and learning has had a real impact on students' instrumental tuition. The department has adopted a supportive approach in encouraging instrumental teachers to use the blogs, as would be expected – their instrumental staff have a wide range of technological abilities. But the use of blogs has quickly spread, mainly as a result of teachers seeing the benefits of their colleagues' blogging, along with the supportive ethos of the department.

A theme throughout this book has been that there are many ways to achieve the same results, and this case study is a perfect example of a department that has experimented and found the best way of achieving their goals. With a DIY attitude, the music staff at Simon Balle have opted to use blogs rather than their VLE to share content with students. Danny explains that this was initially due to their previous VLE being unintuitive and not up to the task.

There have been surprising benefits to the use of public blogs rather than a secure VLE. Although the blogs were initially created to support students at the school, they have also found an unexpected wider audience from across the globe. The main blog receives thousands of hits from outside the school, and Danny is frequently contacted by visitors with questions or thanks for creating the content on the blogs. Many of these visitors are music teachers from other schools who teach A-level Music Technology, who find the blog useful as a source of resources and professional development.

Sharing the content publicly rather than securing it within a VLE has brought great benefits, but taking this route means that the department has to be mindful of child protection and internet safety. When students enter Simon Balle School, their parents are asked for permission for their images to be shared, and this allows the department to post video content featuring students (providing their full names aren't shared along with it). As with any activity, teacher discretion is crucial; the department has to balance carefully the need for student safety with the benefits to learning and engagement that public sharing has brought.

(Phone interview with Danny Fisher, 20th October 2011)

OTHER ONLINE TOOLS

Similar to the advances in creating and recording music, computer programming has also become more democratised. It's now possible for anybody to create their own apps for computers and mobile devices, with a little time and effort. As a result, there's now a huge ecosystem of online music tools that have relevance to the classroom, and the number available is growing steadily.

The real benefit of such tools is that no software needs to be installed to use them. This obviously has benefits in the classroom – as you don't need to pay for or install software on school computers – but additionally makes it easier for students' learning to continue outside of school, on their own mobile devices and computers at home.

This section will take a look at a few of the best online music tools that are relevant to the classroom, along with some tips for finding new ones. As with mobile apps, the tools available online are fairly transient; they tend to come and go as their creators move on to new projects or lose interest in maintaining them. The tools mentioned below are well-established and should stand the test of time.

ONLINE RESOURCE

Quick video tours of the tools mentioned below are provided on the book website, along with short reviews of other online tools. Visit www.rhinegoldeducation.co.uk/dm and use the code ZA6F3W.

INUDGE (www.inudge.net)
iNudge is a step sequencer that presents students with a grid of blocks. Clicking on these blocks allows students to build up ostinatos, and different patterns can be created on top of one another using different instruments (including drums).

All of the available pitches have been devised to work together musically (they're mainly pentatonic). The iNudge can make for a great teaching tool, and students find it addictive!

iNudge can be embedded into a VLE or blog, presenting students with an engaging way of being able to interact with and create music on a department's online space. Once students have created a composition, iNudge also allows them to share it with others, including sending it directly to Facebook for their friends to listen to.

 CLASSROOM IDEA

The fact that iNudge compositions can be easily shared in a number of ways can be very useful if you want to use this tool as the basis for a homework activity. For example:

1. Load iNudge onto the IWB during a lesson, and use it to discuss what makes an effective composition, exploring elements such as rhythm, melody and texture.
2. Give students the task of using iNudge to create their own composition for homework. Set clear success criteria (generated from the class discussion) to ensure that students really think musically when creating their compositions.
3. Ask your students to share their compositions once they have been created. They could email the weblink to you using the built-in email form, or post the link onto a blog or VLE page.
4. During the next lesson, pick a selection of students' compositions and play them back on the IWB. Discuss how well they work, drawing on the success criteria that was created as part of the initial class discussion.
5. It's also possible to build on and edit students' compositions once they've been loaded onto the IWB, which can further extend the activity. Students could load up each others' compositions, for instance, and add further parts or remix them.

MONKEY MACHINE (www.rinki.net/pekka/monkey)
This is a simple drum machine that allows for beats to be built up using an on-screen grid. It's particularly useful when used in conjunction with an interactive white board, and it works well with the classroom idea on page 45. For an online tool it's fairly comprehensive; numerous sets of sounds can be selected, from rock kits to drum machines.

AVIARY (http://advanced.aviary.com)

Aviary is a set of online tools that mimic the functions of previously expensive computer applications, and their features are impressive when you consider that they run completely in an internet browser. Aviary provide two music tools: the audio editor Myna and a grid-based composition tool called Roc.

Myna is perhaps the more interesting of the two, as it is a comprehensive sequencing tool that can be used to record and edit sound, as well as mixing and adding effects to audio. In the past, when a student undertook a sequencing project at school they often weren't able to continue their work at home as the necessary software was too expensive. With tools such as Myna, however, students can simply open their recording at home and continue working on it from any device, which can be a great way of encouraging them to continue their learning at home.

 CLASSROOM IDEA

As Myna is primarily based on loops – students create compositions by building up pre-composed loops of sound rather than writing original material – it's important to ensure that students have a clear musical focus when working with this tool. For example, Myna can be great for allowing students to explore texture and structure, as its loop-based nature means that students can focus purely on these elements.

1. After studying different musical structures with your students, introduce them to the Myna tool and show them how to add loops to build up a composition.

2. Pick a handful of different structures (such as binary, ternary and rondo), and assign them to different students.

3. Ask students to create compositions that make use of these structures. Encourage them to think about the coherence between different sections. Stress that although the focus is on the structure of the composition, it's also important for the music to be effective and enjoyable.

4. At the end of the activity, listen back to a selection of compositions. Ask students to guess which structure has been used in each, explaining the reasons why.

GAMELAN MECANIQUE
(http://www.citedelamusique.fr/gamelan/shock.html)

There are a number of free 'virtual gamelan' sites on the internet, and this is definitely one of the higher quality and more comprehensive ones. One thing you'll notice when you visit the site is that it's all in French, with no English translations provided. However, the high-quality images and sounds, coupled with the intuitive controls, make it very easy to operate.

The beauty of this site is the richness of the experience: 'playing' the gamelan is a responsive, satisfying and most importantly musical experience. The colour-coding of the notes and the ability to mute different instruments also helps you to really make sense of the different layers and structures in the music.

 CLASSROOM IDEA

The following idea is just one example of how this website can be used to explore the main features of gamelan music.

1. In groups, ask students to access the website on a computer or mobile device.
2. Provide each group with the notes of the pentatonic scale that is used in the two pieces from Java. (Although it is impossible to translate gamelan music directly into Western tuning, it is easy enough to work out rough approximations.)
3. Ask each group to try to recreate a performance of one of the two pieces from Java, using instruments such as glockenspiels, keyboards and cymbals. Students could mute or play individual instruments to work out their parts. Alternatively, they could read the grid-based notation provided on the website (which colour codes all of the notes).
4. As a result of this activity, students should have achieved a basic grasp of the key features of gamelan music. Load up the website onto the IWB and use it as part of a class discussion to consolidate their understanding further. How is the music structured? How do the different instruments relate to each other? What are the main features of the core melody? How is it elaborated? Answering these questions will help your students to draw up a list of characteristic features of Javanese gamelan music.
5. Students could then use this list as a basis for their own gamelan compositions. They might want to input their music into the grid section of

the website (although note that there is no function to save your work here). Students could even draw a graphical representation of their own composition, as has been done for the pieces on the website.

AUDIOTOOL (http://www.audiotool.com)

Audiotool is the most advanced of the web tools covered in this section; it is hard to believe that such a fully featured tool is able to run completely within a browser! Audiotool is loaded with a bank of virtual representations of music-technology devices, such as drum machines, synthesisers, mixers, effects boxes and sequencers – each with their own controls, buttons and switches.

These devices can be linked up on screen, allowing students to create their own compositions with almost unlimited possibilities. As a starting point, it's worth first asking students to experiment with the demo pieces that are provided, to get a feel for the devices and the ways in which they can be linked.

FINDING ONLINE RESOURCES

The key to navigating the sea of online music tools is to have patience, try out as many as you can, and make a note of the most useful ones. It can actually be quite a fun process, as many of these tools are creative in their approach and can be more innovative and engaging than mainstream tools. The following tips should help to point you in the right direction when you're embarking on a hunt for new tools.

SEARCH ENGINES

Because of the sheer number of tools that are out there, some thought needs to go into exactly what to search for when trying to find new music tools. Including the word 'online' in a search is a good idea as it will help to focus the search on tools that can be accessed from a browser (such as 'online sequencer'). Searching for 'best online music tools' will bring up a number of websites or blogs that list and review tools that should be helpful to you.

TEACHING FORUMS AND BLOGS

These can also be a useful place to look for ideas as they will lead you to recommendations from other music teachers. The tips in the next chapter will help you to find online communities of music teachers, and it's well worth asking for suggestions on music teaching forums (as well as sharing your own experiences!). You should find that Teaching Music (www.teachingmusic.org.uk) is an excellent source of tried and tested online tools for the music classroom. (This website is described in more detail on page 106.)

SOCIAL NETWORKING

Of all the technologies to emerge in recent years, social networking has had one of the biggest impacts. From teenagers to pensioners, it's being used to allow people to connect in a way that wasn't possible before. Because of this widespread usage, many musicians now use Facebook as one of the main ways to promote their music and spread the word about concerts.

Many schools are starting to see Facebook as a valuable way of spreading their message and engaging with the local community, and a number of examples of schools using it well are starting to emerge. Throughout this book we have looked at some of the ways in which music departments can tap into how music happens in the wider world, and Facebook presents a great opportunity to promote school concerts in the same way that professional musicians do.

 CLASSROOM IDEA

CREATE A FACEBOOK EVENT

This is quite a simple idea, but it's a useful way of promoting school concerts. Facebook allows for 'events' to be created, which can feature photos and videos alongside logistical information. Visitors to the event can then click to say that they're attending, which in turn promotes the event among their friends when it appears in their news feed. This digital word of mouth can result in wider awareness of music-department events. It can work especially well for popular-music events such as rock concerts, battle of the bands and DJ gigs.

Like any online tool, Facebook requires an amount of thought and discretion on your part to ensure that it's used as safely as possible. To help keep things safe and professional, you should consider the following:

- Make sure you're familiar with Facebook and how it works before trying to set up an event.

- Don't associate your personal Facebook account with the event. Set up a new account for the purposes of creating and maintaining the event, and use this exclusively.

- Avoid any dialogue with students via the site.

- Check with your school that they're happy for you to use social networking for this purpose before setting up the event.

ONLINE RESOURCE

A video guide that demonstrates how to create a Facebook event is provided on the book website.

As an aside, it's always a good idea to ensure that your personal profile on Facebook is locked down and unviewable to students, especially as the options on the privacy page have often been known to change. Most teaching unions have guides available on their websites that provide information on how you can protect your privacy to avoid any issues. Many schools have also developed their own social-networking policies to help keep both staff and students safe.

ONLINE PROFESSIONAL DEVELOPMENT

In many schools, music teachers are finding that funding is drying up for the day courses they were once able to attend. Even when off-site courses are an option, music teachers often comment that while it's good to get out of school for a day and have a nice lunch, they find it difficult to implement ideas in their own classrooms once they return.

Many teachers are now following a DIY approach to professional development, using the power of the internet to seek out other educators to share ideas and good practice. Classroom ideas and resources have the most value when they come from real teachers in real classrooms, and this is one of the key benefits of using the internet for the purpose of professional development, as the majority of online resources have been developed as a result of actual classroom practice.

Another benefit of online professional development is that it offers a little and often approach, which many teachers find much more effective in developing their practice than the out of school training-day approach.

This section outlines the main tools that you can use to network and develop your classroom skills, along with some tips for getting to grips with online networking and making the most of it as a music educator.

TWITTER (www.twitter.com)

There's little doubt that most readers of this book will have heard of Twitter, but in many cases any real knowledge of it may be quite limited. While it's true that many users' tweets border on the banal, this usually isn't true of the education community! Twitter has become one of the main ways for educators from across the world to network, share good practice and advance their professional development at their own pace.

Twitter can be a confusing place when visited for the first time. Due to the short messages that are exchanged, and the conversations that take place, things move quickly and it's easy to get intimidated by the sheer amount of data that's passing by. But this can be overcome with a little practice and perseverance.

THE BASICS OF TWITTER

- **Tweets:** a 'tweet' is a message that can be up to 140 characters long. These messages are publicly viewable, and people use them to express opinions, comment on recent events, provide an update of what they're up to and so on.

- **Following:** when you 'follow' a user, their tweets will show up in your timeline (the main screen of Twitter once you've logged in). Following users that share your interests allows you to ensure that the messages you see are relevant and interesting to you. Choosing the right people to follow is the key to getting the most from Twitter, and tips on finding people to follow are given below.

- **Hashtags (#):** these are used to 'tag' tweets, and allow other users who are interested in a particular topic to find tweets that are relevant to it. For example, the hashtag for UK education is #ukedchat. If you write a tweet and include #ukedchat in it somewhere, the tweet will appear on the timeline for that hashtag. This timeline presents all of the tweets that have been tagged with #ukedchat (i.e. any tweets that users think are interesting and relevant to UK education).

- **The @ symbol:** it's possible to direct a tweet at a particular user by typing the @ symbol immediately followed by their username. The author, for instance, can be reached at @jamesrcross. Tweets that include the @ symbol are still publicly viewable, but they're a good way to get the attention of one particular user.

FINDING AND FOLLOWING PEOPLE

The steps below will help you to find the right people to follow on Twitter:

1. Create an account, log in and use the search box to search for #musicedchat or #edchatuk. This will give you a list of recent tweets featuring those educational hashtags.

2. Pick a few users that look interesting and follow them. This is done by clicking on their name or photo, which takes you to their profile page, then clicking 'Follow'.

3. After adding a few users, look at their tweets on your timeline. This is a good opportunity to practise keeping up with tweets, but it's also a great way of

discovering other users who you might be interested in following. Look for who they converse with (i.e. who they use the @ symbol to direct tweets to), and if they seem interesting, follow them too. Repeat this process for those users and so on, and you'll quickly find that you've got a growing timeline of tweets.

4. It's best to take it steady and make sure you only follow relevant people, rather than trying to follow as many users as you can find. Carefully curating who you follow is the best way to make sure that Twitter is as effective as possible in supporting your professional development.

ONLINE RESOURCE

A video guide that demonstrates how to use Twitter is available on the book website. We have also provided a list of people in the music-education world who have an online presence via Twitter or a blog; this is not exhaustive but should provide a good place to start when looking for relevant people to connect with online.

TIPS FOR TEACHERS

- Twitter is all about interaction, so don't be afraid to add to the conversation. On the whole, Twitter is a friendly and supportive space, especially within the educational community that uses it.

- Announce yourself! Use the hashtag to make yourself known to the community. A quick tweet saying something along the lines of, 'Hi everybody. I'm a music teacher and I'm new to Twitter #musicedchat' is a great way of beginning to find supportive followers.

- Be aware that your tweets are publicly viewable, and that your students will potentially be able to see them. Common sense and caution is needed, so keep the conversation professional and positive. It is possible to make your profile private, but using this option makes it much more difficult to build an effective network.

- Most smartphones have apps that allow you to browse your tweets on the go, and this can be one of the easiest ways to keep up with Twitter and the rapid flow of tweets.

TEACHMEETS (www.teachmeet.org.uk)

TeachMeets are free informal events where teachers get together for show-and-tell type sessions. They're very much linked to the online world, as they were conceived by tweeting educators and are organised using Twitter and other online tools.

Many teachers who attend a TeachMeet comment that it's the best CPD they've experienced, because the ideas presented are from real teachers who've used them in their classrooms. Often teachers who are presenting will also share their resources online, meaning that ideas can be used straight away in the classroom by others.

Like the Twitter community, the TeachMeet community is friendly and welcoming, and presenting an idea of your own at a TeachMeet is a great way of networking and meeting like-minded teachers. It's equally fine to sit back and just be inspired by other teachers' talks. It's even possible to attend TeachMeets virtually, by watching live video streams from events across the country and using Twitter hashtags to add to the conversation.

To attend a TeachMeet, visit www.teachmeet.org.uk and look down the page to find one that's nearby. Clicking on the name of a TeachMeet will take you through to a sign-up form to attend or present. There's often a TeachEat afterwards at a nearby restaurant, to continue the conversations and networking.

TEACHING MUSIC (www.teachingmusic.org.uk)

Teaching Music has quickly become the main online space for music teachers in the UK to share their experiences and resources, and to network with each other. It features a comprehensive resource bank that can be a great timesaver for the busy music teacher, as it allows you to access ready-made resources that can be adapted for use in your own classroom.

The site also features a forum that allows music teachers to post questions and contribute to discussions. Topics in the forum range from thoughts on how to best teach notation to useful iPad apps, and the community is very friendly and supportive. If you are looking to make your first step into online professional networking, this is a good place to start.

Members can also be searched for by geographical area, so it's a good space for networking with teachers who are located in nearby schools. As each member has their own profile and blog that they can update, it's also a great way for you to create a professional online presence.

BLOGGING

Many of the links to resources that are shared on Twitter originate from teachers' blogs. These blogs are generally used to share ideas from within the classroom and to reflect on teaching experiences. Music teachers who have professional blogs find that it can be a great way of maintaining their enthusiasm, networking with other music educators, and improving their classroom practice by reflecting on what works best.

Starting a professional blog is a straightforward process: you can follow the same steps outlined on page 91. It's then just a case of committing to update the blog regularly and inviting others to read it. It's also possible for visitors to comment on blog posts, and encouraging readers to do so is a good way of extending your blog into a two-way conversation (as well as confirming that people are reading your posts!).

A blog can also have other professional benefits. If you are applying for new teaching posts or promotions within school, a blog can be a powerful demonstration that you are innovative, committed to your own professional development, and dedicated to providing the best learning experiences for your students.

Blogging platforms have evolved to a point where they're very easy to use, and the main challenge is coming up with content and dedicating time to writing. But you are likely to find that it becomes a rewarding habit, especially when it results in constructive conversations with other music educators.

TIPS FOR TEACHERS

- Keep your blog professional and use your common sense regarding what's appropriate to blog about; moaning about the head teacher or naming specific students is likely to land you in hot water!

- Keep your posts short and concise. Blog posts formatted with bullet points tend to work well and are easy to read; ideas such as 'five tips for managing behaviour in the music classroom' or 'ten tips for newly qualified music teachers' lend themselves well to this type of format.

- Promote your blog! Twitter comes in useful here, as you can simply paste a link to your latest post in a tweet, to let your band of followers know they should check it out. You'll be adding value to the community by sharing your experiences, which will be welcomed by others.

- Encourage visitors to leave a comment; including a couple of questions at the end of your post can be a great way of doing this.

SCHOOL RESTRICTIONS

Every school is different, and this can be especially true when it comes to the various internet sites and technologies on access within the school gates. Many of you will find that you're unable to make use of some of the technologies and web tools mentioned in this book due to internet filtering or restrictive school policies. This can be a significant barrier to innovation, and it often stops teachers from being able to try the things they'd like to.

However, the situation is slowly beginning to change: more schools are starting to experiment with handheld devices, and online tools are increasingly becoming a key learning resource. Schools are also becoming more independent, with an increasing ability to set their own policies and agendas when it comes to teaching and learning.

It's an exciting time if you are enthusiastic about using digital media in your classroom, but you will often still have to navigate challenges in order to introduce innovative technologies. There are two issues that stand out in particular: internet filtering (which results in certain websites being blocked from view), and the use of mobile devices (particularly when this involves students' own phones). These can present something of a minefield, with e-safety issues, school policies and internal politics adding to the mix.

The aim of this chapter is to equip you with some strategies and tools that you can use to help overcome these restrictions. Of course every school will have their own unique challenges and circumstances, but there's one constant that needs to be kept in mind, which is the musical learning. Any request to trial a new technology or technique in the classroom should be squarely focused on the learning outcomes of your students. If you can make a strong case for how your students' learning will benefit, this should lead to a successful outcome.

There are typically two sets of decision makers when it comes to digital media in schools: technical staff (such as network managers) and school leaders (at both the senior leadership and middle leadership levels).

PERSUADING NETWORK MANAGERS

The attitude of school technicians varies from school to school. On one end of the scale are the technicians who understand that the learning should come first, and are happy to help you in an open-minded way. On the opposite end of the scale are the gatekeepers, who will meet many requests with arguments that it 'just can't be done'.

Music teachers and network managers occupy different worlds and it can be useful to take a moment to consider the jobs that they do, and how this impacts on their motivations and priorities. Managing a school network is a demanding and often thankless job, and is commonly done on a shoestring with little funding available. Despite this, network managers are expected to meet very high standards in terms of reliability, even when they find themselves understaffed and working with ageing kit.

Consider then what they might think when you approach and ask for YouTube to be unblocked. They're likely to wonder what impact this will have on the network and its performance for the rest of the school. They'll wonder how long it would take them to implement such a change and how this fits with their other priorities. They'll also wonder how student safety issues will be addressed, and whether there'll be any backlash for them if there are issues. In many cases, the combination of these factors will amount to a 'sorry, it just can't be done', leaving you feeling deflated and unable to innovate.

However, considering their point of view will make it easier for you to present effective proposals and this, combined with a few tools and a little charm, can go a long way in helping you to achieve your technological goals. Building a positive relationship with network managers and technicians can be the single most effective way of getting what you want when it comes to technology.

REQUEST A CHANGE ON A NO-RISK, TRIAL BASIS

This is a sales technique that is often used by retailers today. They allow you to buy or order an item with the promise that if you don't like it, you can easily return it for free, meaning there's no risk to the customer. This significantly increases sales as it makes customers more willing to try out a new product, but very few of them go to the effort of returning it afterwards.

You can also use this technique when dealing with network managers. By carefully pitching your proposition to include a no-risk element, you can increase your chances of getting your proposal accepted. Here are some suggestions:

1. When you approach a network manager with a request, emphasise from the start that you're only looking to carry it out on a trial basis (three weeks is a good timeframe to aim for, as it's long enough to trial a piece of technology properly, but short enough to sound like a manageable length of time).

2. Ask to meet up and discuss the results after the trial, when you can assess where to go next (this is key as it doesn't require any commitment beyond those three weeks).

3. Use the technology for this time period and document specific learning outcomes that you see as a result of using it, along with anything else that might help your case.

4. At the end of the three weeks, get in touch and ask to meet up to discuss the outcome. Technicians are busy people, and if there haven't been any issues with the trial then they'll often be happy for it to continue.

MAKE IT SMALL-SCALE

While it might be nice to have YouTube available across the entire school, it's usually best in the first instance to ask for a change to be made only in the music department. This helps to negate any fears on the part of the technicians that the network might become overloaded, and it also allows for the music department to foster a sense of trust when asking for new resources. If the department has previously had resources installed and unblocked and no issues have come of it, it makes it all the more likely that future requests will be accepted with less resistance.

PERSUADING SCHOOL LEADERS

Of all the tools covered in this book, the most common sticking point when it comes to gaining approval from school leaders concerns the use of mobile devices in the classroom. Many schools have blanket policies with regard to students' own mobile devices, and zero-tolerance approaches are still common.

The rationale behind these stances makes sense on the surface: mobiles have the potential to be hugely disruptive to learning, and blanket bans on them are an effective way of maintaining order in the classroom. But mobile devices have come a long way since many of these bans were implemented; they're now fully fledged computers and the possibilities for learning with them have increased dramatically.

MAKE A CASE FOR THE LEARNING

What goes on in the music classroom can often be something of a mystery to senior school leaders, and if you add mobile devices into the mix it can be even more difficult for them to picture exactly how the learning will happen. For this reason, it's essential that you are explicit about exactly how the learning will be improved if mobile devices are used, and the best way of doing this is to paint a series of pictures in their minds around specific scenarios.

The 'mobile devices' chapter on pages 55–71 contains lots of ideas that can be adapted for this purpose. You could pick a few examples that are specific to your classroom to present to school leaders. A selection of three or four contrasting examples should do the job nicely, demonstrating how mobile devices will be used in different scenarios and by different types of student.

PRE-EMPT ANY CONCERNS

It's likely that school leaders will raise some valid concerns when it comes to the use of mobile devices in the classroom, and it's helpful to have some responses ready. Some of the more common concerns are listed below, along with a response that can be given to help reassure school leaders.

'How will you manage their use?'

It won't be a free-for-all: students will need to ask permission to use a mobile device, and will need to explain to the teacher specifically how they'll be using it for their learning. The focus will always be on using devices responsibly for learning.

'Won't they be texting/calling/using Facebook instead of working?'

This is very easily spotted, and if students are found to be doing this, they'll lose the chance to use their devices for learning. The responsible use of mobiles for learning will be encouraged, while the normal rules and procedures for classroom disruption will apply when students misbehave with the devices.

'If we let students use their mobiles in Music lessons, surely they'll expect to use them in other subjects too, causing disruption?'

Before students use their mobiles in Music, it will be made clear to them that they're *only* allowed to use their devices in Music, and only for specific purposes, with the teacher's permission. They'll be reminded that the normal school rules still apply elsewhere.

'What about students who don't have their own devices?'

It's important that students who don't have mobile devices aren't made to feel embarrassed or excluded in any way. The ways in which devices are used in the classroom will be planned sensitively, with this in mind. Activities that require every student to have a device will be avoided (unless the school is able to provide class sets). In most cases, students' use of devices will be on an ad-hoc basis as part of group work, so that students can be sensitively grouped where access to a mobile device may be needed.

THREE REASONS THAT SCHOOLS SHOULD...

UNBLOCK YOUTUBE

1. It's one of the biggest (free) educational resources ever, and it's an important part of learning in the world of music. If students don't have access to this in school, their learning is being let down.

2. Issues about student safety have now been addressed by YouTube, with a new filtering option that allows students to access only educational content during lessons.

3. The responsible use of YouTube for learning should be encouraged, and if students are taught to use it positively in school, it'll help them to learn independently outside the school gates.

ALLOW MOBILE DEVICES FOR LEARNING

1. Students have devices in their pockets that are powerful tools for learning, which will stay with them throughout their educational and working lives. Instead of ignoring these devices, it's important that schools teach students to use them responsibly to help their learning.

2. They add to the ICT provision that the school provides, allowing wider access to information.

3. With high expectations and a focus on responsible use, any potential disruption can easily be managed, and is far outweighed by the potential for learning.

COPYRIGHT

Copyright has always presented something of a minefield to music teachers, and as technologies have evolved, boundaries have become much less clear-cut. New technologies allow for music to be shared, discussed and remixed with ease, but the music industry often finds itself at odds with consumers' behaviour around online music. Things have started to improve recently as innovative legitimate services such as iTunes and Spotify have arrived, and the tactic of legal action against the music-downloading consumer has fallen out of favour. However, music licensing has become increasingly complex and this is especially true when it comes to its use in the classroom.

It is difficult to give concrete and definitive advice here, as the landscape (with its grey areas and muddy waters) evolves rapidly as new technologies and services develop. That said, the best way for you to protect yourself when making use of digital media is to ensure that the owner has given permission for its use and distribution.

CREATIVE COMMONS

Creative Commons is a licensing scheme that allows content creators to give others permission to use and alter their works for creative purposes. Millions of songs, videos and photographs are available under a Creative Commons licence. In the majority of cases, works licensed in this way can be downloaded, distributed, remixed and adapted freely, as long as it's for non-commercial use and the original author is credited when the work is shared.

There's an easy-to-use search feature at http://search.creativecommons.org, which allows you to search for different types of digital media that you can use in your classroom. This webpage acts as a gateway to other content providers, highlighting material that can be used freely and adapted without any copyright worries.

As Creative Commons continues to spread, a growing number of sites are adding features that allow media to be shared under this licence.

VIMEO (www.vimeo.com)

Vimeo is a site that's much like YouTube but with a focus on original creative works. Many of the videos on Vimeo are Creative Commons licensed, and this is signified by the Creative Commons logo appearing in small print on the video page, just below the video itself. In most cases, this allows you to download the video and use it as you wish (clicking on the logo brings up the exact licensing terms for that video).

SOUNDCLOUD (www.soundcloud.com)

SoundCloud is a creative music-sharing community for musicians. It has a section of tracks licensed under Creative Commons that can be found at www.soundcloud.com/creativecommons.

CCMIXTER (www.ccmixter.org)

This is an online community of remixers that offers Creative Commons licensed samples and a capella vocal tracks for creative use.

INTERNET ARCHIVE (www.archive.org)

This site offers a wide range of Creative Commons works for download, and its video selection is particularly useful for classroom composition projects.

GLOSSARY

Amplifier (amp). A device that allows the sound of an instrument (often the electric guitar) to be made considerably louder.

Adapter. A device that converts one type of connection to another. A well-known everyday example is the travel adapter, which allows you to connect a British plug to an American socket (for example). The most commonly used adapter in the music classroom is one that converts small headphone jacks to large ones.

Application (app). A computer program that has been packaged up in a format that allows it to be easily downloaded and installed. The term is most used to refer to the small computer programs that often cost no more than a few pounds, which are designed to be downloaded to a mobile device.

App store. An online catalogue of applications, which can be purchased and installed on a mobile device or computer with a few simple clicks.

Audacity. An audio editing program, which can be used on both the Mac and PC. See page 41 for more information.

Blog. A type of website that allows users to update it regularly with content, which is presented in chronological order. While blogs started out as simple online diaries, many have now evolved to be fully-featured websites in their own right. See page 85 for more information.

Broadband. A high-speed method of connecting to the internet. Most homes in the UK now have broadband internet.

Condenser microphone. The type of microphone most often used in recording studios, as its sensitivity means that it can capture a clear and nuanced sound. However, unlike some other microphones, it requires a power supply to use. Many **USB microphones** are condenser microphones, as a USB connection can offer the necessary power.

Creative Commons. A licensing scheme that allows content creators (such as composers, photographers and filmmakers) to allow others to legally download, share and adapt their work, often on the condition that it is for non-commercial purposes. See page 115 for more information.

Cubase. A **sequencing** program with a long history of use in UK schools. It is essentially a virtual studio that allows you to record, edit, arrange and mix sounds on your computer.

Digital video camera. A small, portable device that allows video to be captured and transferred directly to computer. (Digital video cameras often incorporate a **USB arm** for this purpose).

Discussion forum. An online space that allows users to contribute to conversations in a written format.

Drum machine. A device that allows users to build up drum patterns, by programming different drum sounds to be triggered along to a beat.

Embedding. The process of taking a piece of content from one website (such as a video from YouTube), and placing it onto another website (such as a blog). See page 75 for more information.

Export. The process of saving a file to a format that allows it to be used by other computers or programs. Many mobile apps, for example, allow users to 'export' material into a generic format that can then be opened on any computer.

Facebook. A **social networking** website that allows users to connect, interact and share media online with people who they already know in real life.

FL Studio. A **sequencing** program that acts as a virtual studio, allowing you to record, edit, arrange and mix sounds on your computer. See page 67 for more information.

Flipchart. An electronic document that can be opened on an interactive whiteboard. It typically includes a variety of media and interactive elements (such as images linked to audio files, which play when you click on them).

Garageband. A **sequencing** program that acts as a virtual studio, allowing you to record, edit, arrange and mix sounds on your computer. It comes free with new Mac computers.

Hard drive. The device within a computer that allows for files to be stored and saved.

High definition (HD). Videos in 'high definition' have a clearer and sharper picture than videos in 'standard definition'. As a result, high-definition video files are also larger in size.

iMovie. A video editing program, which comes free with new Mac computers.

Import. The process of bringing existing content into a computer program. For example, footage from a video camera would need to be 'imported' into a video editing program in order to edit it.

Interactive whiteboard (IWB). A device that projects documents and web pages onto a large, interactive screen. It is possible to manipulate documents on the screen by touch (for example, you can drag objects around the screen with your fingers, or touch a video to play it).

iNudge. An online **step sequencer** tool, which allows for pentatonic compositions to be built up by clicking on a series of blocks. See page 95 for more information.

iOS. The operating system that Apple's mobile devices, such as the iPhone and iPad, run on.

iPad. A **tablet** computer, manufactured by Apple.

iPhone. A **smartphone**, manufactured by Apple.

iPod. A range of music players, manufactured by Apple, with varying functionality – from simple music playback to more advanced smartphone-like features.

iPod Touch. An iPod that is similar in design and functionality to an iPhone, which allows you to browse the web and download apps.

iTunes. A program that allows you to play music and video. It also incorporates a large digital store, where video and music can be purchased.

Mac. A brand of computer, manufactured by Apple, that runs the OS X operating system.

Memory card. A small, portable device that is used to store data. For example, it can be slotted into a digital video camera, allowing you to store the footage captured. It can then be taken out and inserted into a computer, allowing you to transfer the footage from the video camera onto the computer.

MIDI. A type of computer language that allows musical devices (such as piano keyboards and sequencing programs) to communicate with each other. For example, MIDI can encode a melody into a series of digital messages, which can then be sent to another device and turned back into sound.

MIDI keyboard. A piano keyboard that has MIDI functionality, which allows it to be connected to other MIDI devices (such as computers or synthesiser modules).

Mixing. The process of bringing together and combining different recorded sounds (or separate tracks). DJs use mixers, for example, to combine the sounds of two record players in a controlled way.

Mobile device. A portable computing device. The term is generally used to refer to **smartphones** and **tablets**.

MP3. A type of sound file that has been compressed to make it easier to share.

MP3 recorder. A portable recording device that incorporates a microphone, which allows sound to be recorded directly to MP3.

Multitracking. The ability to layer up multiple lines of sound when recording a piece. For example, a band will be recorded in a studio using this method: guitars, vocals, bass and drums are recorded onto separate tracks that can be manipulated individually before being brought together.

MySpace. A **social networking** website that peaked in popularity around 2008. Although it is now dwarfed by Facebok, MySpace is often credited with starting the social networking revolution. It is popular with musicians who use it as a marketing tool.

Napster. The original version of Napster was a service that allowed users to freely (and often illegally) share music files with each other. Napster changed the music industry forever, leading to the foundation of legal music streaming services such as **Spotify**.

NUMU. A website that allows schools to create their own 'record label', to which students and teachers can safely upload and share audio content that they have created. See page 40 for more information.

Omnidirectional microphone. A microphone that picks up sound from every direction.

Playlist. A collection of songs or videos that a user has put together, generally with a specific theme or purpose (such as a playlist of videos about recording techniques).

Podcast. A regular series of audio (or video) content that can be subscribed to by users. Podcasts frequently take the form of an **MP3** file that can be downloaded onto a mobile device (the word is an amalgamation of 'broadcast' and 'iPod', referring to the fact that it developed as a type of broadcasting that involved users downloading content to their iPods).

Remixing. The process of taking an existing piece of media (such as music or video), and manipulating it to create something new and original.

Rich media. Media that includes video or audio, or some form of interaction, as opposed to purely text-based content.

Sequencer. A device or program that allows users to record and edit music to build up a composition.

Skype. A program that allows users to make telephone and video calls between two or more computers, using the internet.

Smartphone. A phone that offers features and functions that go way beyond the ability to make calls and send text messages. Most of the additional features result from the ability to connect to the internet and download **apps**.

Social network. A type of website that allows users to share content and connect with each other. **Facebook** and **Twitter** are the most well-known social networks.

Sound card. The device within a computer that allows for sound to be played.

Spotify. A music streaming service, which allows users to listen to a huge collection of music without having to download it to their computers.

Step sequencer. A type of composition tool based on a grid, which allows users to create music by selecting a series of blocks (or steps) in the grid.

Streaming. The process of playing a piece of media (usually video or audio) while being connected to the internet; this allows you to play the media without having to download it first.

Synthesiser. A device that is capable of creating sounds from scratch, often by manipulating basic types of sound wave. Synthesisers can emulate existing instruments, but can also produce their own unique sounds.

Tablet. A thin, ultra-portable computer. It usually doesn't have a keyboard – the main feature instead is the large **touch screen** that often spans its entire surface.

Touch screen. A screen that allows you to interact with elements in a document or web page by touch. In effect, touching the screen with your fingers (or a pen) replaces the concept of clicking with a mouse. Touch screens are the main way of interacting with smartphones and tablets.

Tumblr. A website that allows users to create and maintain a **blog**. See page 91 for more information.

Twitter. A **social networking** website that is based around short text updates. See page 103 for more information.

USB port. A connection point on a computer that allows you to plug in devices to it (such as a printer or digital video camera).

USB arm. This is a feature of many digital video cameras and MP3 recorders, which allows them to be plugged directly into a computer (via its **USB port**) without the need for a separate cable.

USB microphone. A microphone that connects directly to the computer via its **USB port**. This direct connection often increases sound quality, and makes the microphone easier to use.

Vimeo. An online video sharing site, similar to **YouTube**, which is popular with film makers and video artists.

Visualiser. A video camera attached to a stand that allows its position to be changed easily. It can be used to display live video on a computer screen or interactive whiteboard.

Virtual Learning Environment (VLE). An online space that all members of a school have access to, allowing them to communicate, share content and make use of online learning tools.

Web 2.0. When the internet first developed, most people used it passively to browse and consume content. Web 2.0 marked the point at which users could interact with the web in more advanced, active ways – such as by creating and publishing their own content, and contributing to social networking sites.

Webcam. A video camera that is connected to a computer, allowing for video conferencing to take place. Many modern laptops have a small webcam built into their screen.

Windows Movie Maker. A video editing program, which comes free with the Windows operating system.

YouTube. A website that allows users to post and share videos.